NETWORK LIKE A PRO

THE ULTIMATE GUIDE TO SUCCESSFUL NETWORKING

Emmelie Forsyth

Description

The value of networking cannot be overstated in today's competitive corporate environment. Building and nurturing strong connections with like-minded individuals can be the trigger for incredible success, whether you're a seasoned professional or a young entrepreneur. "Network Like a Pro: The Ultimate Guide to Successful Networking" is a thorough and invaluable eBook that will provide you with the knowledge, skills, and techniques you need to handle networking opportunities like a genuine expert.

Inside this carefully produced guide, you'll find a treasure trove of practical advice, tried-and-true strategies, and insider secrets that will transform your approach to networking. This eBook, written by industry insiders and networking experts, serves as your mentor, taking you by the hand and guiding you through the intricacies of networking with confidence and grace. "Network Like a Pro" equips you with the tools you need to transform networking from a frightening activity into an exhilarating voyage of personal and professional growth, whether you're attending a conference, a trade fair, or a professional event. This eBook is ideal for professionals aiming to advance their careers, entrepreneurs looking to build their businesses, and anybody wishing to realize the actual power of networking in today's linked world.

Foreword

Embracing the Power of a Smile and Connection

In the bustling world of business development and advertising, I've had the privilege of travelling the globe, attending countless conferences, tradeshows and events, and meeting an astonishing array of individuals – from high-flying CEOs to eager interns just starting their journey. Throughout my 15+year career, I have passionately embraced the power of networking, a practice that has become the cornerstone of my success and, more importantly, a source of genuine fulfilment.

As I look back on the remarkable path I've travelled, I find myself awestruck by the incredible network I've built. But what truly warms my heart are the many friendships that have blossomed from these professional connections. This e-book is a testament to the incredible potential that lies within the simple act of connecting with fellow humans, regardless of their status in the business world.

"You never know where a conversation will take you" – a phrase that has become my mantra. And it is more than just a catchy slogan; it's a profound belief that has shaped my entire approach to networking. At every conference, I have made it a point to engage with people, listen to their stories, and share my own experiences openly. Whether I'm full of energy or exhausted from jet lag, I understand that every conversation holds the potential to lead to something extraordinary.

The magic of networking lies in its ability to transcend professional boundaries and reveal the common thread that unites us all as humans. Every connection forged, no matter how brief, has the potential to enrich our lives in ways we can scarcely imagine. It's a reminder that, behind the titles and the corporate jargon, we are all on a shared journey, seeking success, happiness, and fulfilment.

A simple smile, a genuine interest in someone's story, a willingness to lend a helping hand – these are the building blocks of powerful connections. Throughout my career, I have learned that authentic relationships are not solely about what we can gain professionally, but about the joy of connecting, sharing, and supporting each other on our respective paths.

This e-book aims to shed light on the transformative power of a smile and genuine connections. It's a celebration of the vast opportunities that emerge when we embrace the mindset of curiosity and empathy in our networking efforts. As you read through these pages, I hope you'll be inspired to approach your networking endeavours with renewed enthusiasm, knowing that every interaction, no matter how seemingly insignificant, can lead to unforeseen possibilities.

So, let us embark on this journey together – a journey of smiles, handshakes, and heartfelt conversations. As you delve into the stories and insights shared within this book, I encourage you to embrace the belief that every person you meet, regardless of their status in the business world, holds the potential to enrich your life in ways you never thought possible.

May the power of a smile and genuine connection guide you on your path to success, both personally and professionally.

With warm regards,

Emmelie

Contents

Introduction

Hello, and welcome to Network Like a Pro, the complete manual for networking at business events. Whether you're an old hand at networking or just starting, this all-in-one guide will give you the skills you need to make the most of "coffee networking breaks."

In the media, entertainment, advertising, and production industries, networking is the key to success, and I'm excited to share all the ways I've learned over the years. But here's the secret: it's not just about sales talks and business cards. Oh, no! It's all about making genuine relationships with other people that last.

I will show you the power of networking and bust some myths holding you back on these pages. Together, we'll help you build a way of thinking about networking to set you up for long-term success. First, we will talk about self-reflection, which will help you figure out your goals, strengths, and unique personal brand. This is a significant first step on your networking path.

Get ready to rock those events where you meet people. We will teach you how to study, make a great elevator pitch, and improve your communication skills so that everyone you meet will remember you.

But guess what? Social media is our playground as well. Together we will learn how to use LinkedIn and look at ways to network virtually, giving you more impact than ever before.

But that's not the end of it! Inside and outside of your company, networking is a superpower. We'll talk about internal networking, working with people from different departments, and the magic of getting to know teachers and leaders.

We'll also talk about problems like being shy, being afraid of being rejected, and being good at social networking. But don't worry; we have helpful ways to beat them all!

This is more than just a book; it's an adventure. I will be there with you, sharing personal stories, thoughts, and tips to help you find your way in the networking world. We'll give you the confidence to connect with anyone, anywhere, no matter your age, gender, or level of experience.

Together, let's open the door to success by turning every chance to network into an opportunity to make friends for life. Get ready to change the game during your coffee breaks.

Welcome to Network Like a Pro, where networking becomes your secret tool in the exciting worlds of media, entertainment, advertising, and production and quite frankly any business and personal sector. Lets dive in!

Chapter 1: The Power of Networking

I would like to take this opportunity to welcome you to "Network Like a Pro: The Ultimate Guide to Successful Networking" As we embark on this journey together, I couldn't be more excited to share my knowledge and experiences with you to assist you in becoming an experienced networker. This book will delve deeply into the networking world, illuminating the latent potential inside seemingly innocuous coffee breaks and industry events.

1.1 Understanding the Benefits

Networking is more than simply exchanging business cards and forming superficial relationships. It involves nurturing genuine interactions and creating a support community within your industry. Networking's power resides in its capacity to open doors and create opportunities you could never have imagined.

Consider the following scenario: During a coffee break at a conference, you converse with a stranger. This individual is a key decision-maker at a company you have always admired. They value your authenticity and feel a connection with you. Who will they remember when their company has a job opening that perfectly matches their skills and aspirations? Indeed, they will recall you because of your favorable impression during that coffee break.

However, the benefits of networking extend beyond landing a position or acquiring a new client. By establishing relationships with others in your industry, you gain access to valuable insights, trends, and confidential information that can give you a competitive advantage. Networking also provides a platform for collaboration and the exchange of knowledge, which leads to the generation of original ideas and inventive problem-solving.

Additionally, networking can improve your self-assurance and communication skills. Conversations with individuals from disparate professional backgrounds enhance your ability to articulate your thoughts and present yourself effectively.

Networking is a potent instrument that can result in career advancements, collaborations, partnerships, and enduring friendships. It's not just about short-term gains; it's also about cultivating relationships that will bear fruit in the long run.

Let's examine some of the thrilling professional and personal benefits that effective networking can bring:

- Gain access to many insights from the industry and emerging trends when you network with professionals from different sectors and experiences. Networking allows you to remain ahead of the curve, make informed choices, and capitalize on new opportunities.
- Collaboration and Synergy: Networking facilitates collaboration and provides opportunities between individuals with similar interests. By engaging in meaningful conversations with others, you may discover complementary skills or expertise that can lead to intriguing partnerships, joint ventures, or projects with a more significant impact than you could accomplish.
- Mentorship and Training: Networking exposes you to seasoned mentors and influential thought leaders who can provide career guidance. Mentors offer invaluable advice, share their experiences, and provide constructive criticism, accelerating professional development.
- Increased Professional Network: A robust network provides access to many connections. The more people you connect with, the larger your network grows, exponentially

increasing your chances of gaining access to various opportunities and resources.

- Networking improves communication and interpersonal skills, which increases your self-confidence. Engaging in meaningful conversations with professionals of varying career levels and backgrounds enables you to articulate your ideas, receive feedback, and develop self-confidence.

- My personal experience, when I was starting out in the industry in London, my Initial hesitation, and severe Imposter syndrome, prevented me from approaching industry executives at conferences. As I gained confidence in my networking abilities, I began engaging in enlightening conversations with fellow delegates of all levels of seniority plus top executives, leading to exciting opportunities and also new friendships from around the world.

- Job Openings and Professional Advancement: Networking is an effective method for locating unadvertised job and career advancement opportunities. You can access exclusive employment opportunities that perfectly match your skills and goals through connections and referrals.

- Personal Satisfaction and Support Group: Creating genuine connections with like-minded people generates a supportive community where you can share your successes and difficulties. Networking fosters alliances that extend beyond the professional realm, providing a sense of belonging and personal satisfaction.

Over the years, I have cultivated a network of individuals who share my enthusiasm for the media and entertainment industries. This community offers unwavering support, celebrates accomplishments, and offers solace during difficult circumstances.

When approached with earnestness and an open mind, networking has the potential to alter your professional journey profoundly. The benefits range from career advancement and industry knowledge to personal fulfillment and enduring friendships. In the following chapters, we will examine how to make the most of networking opportunities by forging genuine connections that elevate your networking skills to an entirely new level. Therefore, let's continue on this path to become a master networker and unlock a universe of opportunities!

1.2 Dispelling Common Networking Myths

Let's discuss how to get the most out of networking opportunities by forging genuine connections that take your networking game to the next level. Therefore, let's continue on this path to become an expert networker. Despite the numerous advantages of networking, several fallacies and misunderstandings frequently prevent individuals from fully embracing this effective practice. Let's debunk these myths and cast light on why some people disregard networking despite its potential to skyrocket their careers.

Myth 1: Networking is inefficient and time-consuming

One of the most widespread misconceptions about networking is its laborious and ineffective nature. Some worry that attending events and participating in conversations will waste their valuable time with little to show. This misunderstanding originates from a misunderstanding of networking's purpose.

Reason: The reality is that networking does not have to be a constant time drag. You can maximize the effects of your networking efforts by employing a strategic and deliberate strategy. Instead of attempting to network with everyone, establish meaningful relationships with key individuals who share your goals and values. Networking can lead to abundant opportunities, making it a highly effective and rewarding endeavor.

Myth. 2: Networking is Transactional and Manipulative

Another common misunderstanding is that networking involves exploiting others for personal benefit or participating in superficial exchanges to advance one's career. This myth portrays networking as a self-serving activity devoid of genuine human connections.

Effective networking is predicated on sincerity and mutual gain. One can cultivate genuine relationships beyond transactional relationships by approaching connecting with an honest interest in getting to know people, comprehending their perspectives, and supporting their goals. Networking entails establishing relationships based on trust and rapport, in which both parties benefit from mutual growth and development.

Myth 3: Networking Is Exclusively for Extroverts

Many individuals avoid networking because they assume it is a trait unique to extroverted individuals. The mistaken belief that networking requires an extroverted and charismatic personality may discourage introverts from attending industry events due to feelings of anxiety.

While extroverts may be naturally drawn to networking, introverts have unique qualities that make them superb networkers. Active listening, profound empathy, and deliberate communication are all valuable traits that introverts can use to establish meaningful relationships. Regardless of personality type, networking is about finding common ground and being open to learning from others.

Myth 4: Networking is limited to conventional events.

Some people presume networking opportunities are restricted to formal industry events and conferences. They may be unaware that networking can occur online and offline.

In the age of technology, networking has expanded to include LinkedIn, social media organizations, and virtual events. Utilizing these digital channels expands networking possibilities beyond the limitations of physical gatherings. As valuable as face-to-face interactions can be, engaging in online discussions, sharing industry insights, and reaching out to like-minded professionals.

Myth. 5: Networking is awkward and intimidating.

Fear of leaving one's comfort zone and engaging strangers inhibits networking for many individuals. The prospect of initiating conversations with prominent industry executives or more experienced individuals may seem intimidating.

Reason: Although it's normal to experience some anxiety when networking, it's essential to realize that everyone has to start somewhere. Like any other talent, networking improves with practice. Start by conversing with approachable individuals, and gradually develop your self-assurance. Networking is about finding common ground and exchanging experiences, not bragging about achievements.

The power of networking can propel your career to greater heights. By dispelling these myths and understanding the true potential of networking, you can embrace the practice with confidence and open doors to intriguing opportunities. In the following chapters, we will explore actionable strategies and techniques to help you conquer the art of networking, ensuring that you maximize every coffee break and industry event. Therefore, let's proceed and discover the secret to networking success and open the doors to a universe of opportunities!

1.3 Building a Networking Mindset

To maximize your networking efforts and improve your networking skills, cultivate a growth-oriented mindset and investigate cutting-edge methods that leverage social media, attitude, and genuine connections. Let's delve deeply into these facets so you can become a networking guru.

Accept the Influence of Social Media Networking

Social networking platforms offer unparalleled chances to expand your professional network and connect with industry colleagues and global influencers in the digital age. LinkedIn is a potent tool for professionals to demonstrate their expertise, create a digital brand, and network with prospective collaborators and employers.

Establishing a Powerful Online Presence: Your LinkedIn profile is a virtual business card and professional identity. Ensure your comprehensive profile includes a professional photo, an engaging summary, and a thorough work history. Share your accomplishments, initiatives, and insights to demonstrate your knowledge and leadership.

Participating in Online Discussions: Interact in industry-related LinkedIn and other social platform discussions, groups, and forums. Contribute insightful observations, pose provocative queries, and interact with the content of others. Being active in these online communities can boost your visibility and entice professionals with similar interests.

Position yourself as a subject matter expert by providing valuable content such as posts, videos, and infographics. Not only does providing practical knowledge to your network demonstrate your expertise, but it also encourages engagement and builds trust among your connections.

Develop an Optimistic Networking Attitude

Your disposition is crucial to your networking success. Adopt a positive and receptive attitude to establish genuine connections that leave a lasting impression.

- Confidence and Friendliness: Display confidence when initiating conversations and be friendly to those seeking to communicate with you. A pleasant expression and genuine interest in the experiences of others can set the stage for a productive networking interaction.
- Learning Enthusiasm: Attend networking events with an appetite for information and a willingness to learn from others. Curiosity and a desire to comprehend diverse perspectives foster deeper relationships and enrich networking opportunities.
- Fearless Follow-Up: Do not be frightened to follow up with your connections after an event or a meaningful interaction. A simple email expressing appreciation and a desire to remain in contact can strengthen your relationship and pave the way for future collaborations.

Develop Genuine Connections

Developing genuine relationships is the foundation of effective networking. Focus on establishing genuine relationships that extend beyond superficial interactions.

- Active Listening and Empathy: Practice active listening and show sincere interest in what others say during conversations. Consider their experiences and points of view, which fosters rapport and trust.
- Shared Goals and Interests: Search for connections with whom you share values, interests, or objectives. Shared

interests provide a solid foundation for relationships that transcend professional boundaries.

- Providing Assistance: The process of networking is a two-way road. Be active in extending help and support to your connections by introducing them to relevant contacts or providing them with valuable resources. This strengthens your relationship and enhances the mutual benefits of networking.

Advantages of cutting-edge networking techniques:

Social networking transcends geographical boundaries, enabling you to establish relationships with professionals from all over the world. This global scope provides access to perspectives and opportunities that may not be available locally.

You establish yourself as a thought leader by sharing valuable content and participating in online conversations. This recognition may result in invites to speak at conferences, contributions to industry publications, and increased visibility as a domain expert.

Personal Branding and Confidence: Cultivating a positive networking attitude increases your confidence and personal brand. Consumers tend to remember and interact with professionals who exude energy and friendliness.

Diverse Collaboration Opportunities: Cultivating authentic connections opens various collaboration opportunities. Collaboration with professionals from diverse backgrounds invigorates your projects and initiatives with new perspectives and creativity.

Utilizing advanced networking strategies and social media platforms may significantly broaden your network and provide access to intriguing opportunities. Developing a positive networking attitude and adopting genuine connections will make you a master networker and propel your career to new heights. In the following chapters, we will discuss how to deal with networking events, create persuasive elevator presentations, and establish connections beyond industry gatherings. Let's continue our quest for networking excellence and unleash your professional network's maximum potential!

Summary

So there you have it - the incredible power of networking! This chapter has been all about realising the energy of genuine human connections. We've built the framework for your networking journey, from refuting common networking myths to adopting a networking attitude. Remember that networking is more than just passing out business cards and making small conversations; it is about developing real contacts that can change your career unexpectedly. So, as you enter the networking world, take a deep breath, be open to new experiences, and let curiosity guide you.

As we progress through this ultimate guide, we'll delve even further into networking at business events and investigate numerous tactics for cultivating long-lasting friendships. So buckle up for a thrilling voyage filled with insights, suggestions, and practical networking skills!

Prepare to open doors, seize opportunities, and leave a memorable impression. Networking is more than a talent; it's a superpower, and you're about to use it to catapult your career to new heights. So, let's get started and enjoy the voyage of networking like a pro. Good luck with your networking, and I'll see you in the next chapter!

"Your network is your net worth." - Porter Gale

Multiple Choice Questions

1. What is the primary power of networking?

a) It helps you make superficial relationships with industry professionals.

b) It allows you to collect as many business cards as possible.

c) It opens doors and creates opportunities you could never have imagined.

d) It guarantees immediate career advancements.

2. What benefits can networking provide beyond landing a job or acquiring new clients?

a) Access to valuable insights, trends, and confidential information.

b) Opportunities for bragging about achievements to others.

c) Guaranteeing long-term friendships and personal satisfaction.

d) Access to exclusive parties and events.

3. Why do some people avoid networking, believing it is time-consuming and inefficient?

a) They misunderstand the purpose of networking.

b) They lack the necessary skills to network effectively.

c) They prefer to work in isolation.

d) They believe networking is only for extroverts.

4. How can introverts be successful networkers despite the common belief that networking is for extroverts?

a) By avoiding industry events and conferences.

b) By approaching networking with an honest interest in getting to know people.

c) By only networking with other introverts.

d) By focusing solely on online networking.

5. What is the key to making networking efforts effective and rewarding?

a) Trying to network with as many people as possible.

b) Building meaningful relationships with key individuals who share your goals and values.

c) Avoiding online networking and sticking to traditional events.

d) Networking only with those in positions of power.

6. How can social media networking platforms, like LinkedIn, benefit networking efforts?

a) They allow you to collect the most business cards.

b) They provide opportunities for superficial interactions.

c) They are inefficient and time-consuming.

d) They enable you to expand your professional network and connect with industry colleagues.

7. What attitude should one adopt to succeed in networking?

a) A self-serving and manipulative attitude.

b) A fear of leaving one's comfort zone.

c) A positive and receptive attitude to establish genuine connections.

d) A focus on bragging about personal achievements.

8. What are some advantages of cutting-edge networking techniques and online engagement?

a) They limit networking to local events and conferences.

b) They provide access to perspectives and opportunities only available in your local area.

c) They allow you to establish relationships with professionals from all over the world.

d) They prevent you from establishing yourself as a thought leader.

9. How does networking improve your self-confidence and personal brand?

a) By collecting as many business cards as possible.

b) By being manipulative and transactional in your interactions.

c) By developing a positive networking attitude and displaying confidence.

d) By avoiding online networking and sticking to face-to-face interactions.

10. What is the ultimate goal of networking, as emphasized in the chapter?

a) To become a master networker and open doors to a universe of opportunities.

b) To make as many superficial connections as possible.

c) To collect business cards from influential individuals.

d) To guarantee immediate career advancements.

Answers

1. c

2. a

3. a, d

4. b

5. b

6. d

7. c

8. c

9. c

10. a

Chapter 2: Building a Strong Foundation

Welcome to Chapter 2 of "Network Like a Pro: The Ultimate Guide to Successful Networking" This chapter will focus on establishing a solid foundation for effective networking. By implementing the ways discussed in this chapter, you will set yourself as a networking powerhouse, obtaining a competitive edge and distinguishing yourself as a true industry professional.

"Networking is not about just connecting people. It's about connecting people with people, people with ideas, and people with opportunities." - Michele Jennae

2.1 Self-Reflection: Knowing Your Goals and Expertise

Self-reflection is a guiding compass in the exciting networking world, leading you to your networking goals and fueling your desire to connect with others. You can launch your networking journey with purpose and clarity by delving deeply into your ambitions, abilities, and experiences.

Understanding Your Networking Objectives:

Networking without a specific goal can feel like meandering aimlessly through a maze of discussions. Before attending any networking event, take a moment to consider what you intend to gain from these contacts. Are you seeking new employment prospects and possible collaborators to broaden your business expertise or build significant mentorship connections?

The Advantages of Having Specific Networking Goals:

Setting specific networking objectives allows you to approach each interaction with focus and resolve. With your goals in mind, you may actively seek out folks who share your goals and establish meaningful and enjoyable conversations. Having a clear sense of direction will transform each networking coffee break into an opportunity for real engagement, whether you're attending a media conference or an advertising summit.

Recognizing Your Competence and Offerings:

We all have unique abilities, experiences, and talents that set us apart professionally. Understanding your area of expertise and what you bring to the table is critical in showing confidence during networking interactions.

The Advantages of Recognizing Your Expertise:

Recognizing your knowledge allows you to establish yourself as a valued asset in any networking situation. Others are more likely to regard you as a competent and trusted professional if you articulate your abilities and accomplishments with authenticity and conviction. Acknowledging your expertise can lead to lecture engagements, collaborations on exciting initiatives, and invitations to exclusive networking circles.

Accepting Your Journey and Growing:

Networking is more than just what you have to offer; it is also about accepting your path and improving. Take pleasure in the obstacles you've faced and the lessons you've learned throughout your career. Embracing your progress and journey gives authenticity to your networking encounters. You make meaningful connections with others when you share your experiences, including victories and setbacks. You motivate individuals around you to be more vulnerable and responsive in their networking encounters by being transparent about your learning process and realizing that progress is a constant endeavor.

Developing Self-Belief and Positive Self-Talk:

Believing in yourself is the secret sauce that takes your networking game from excellent to outstanding. Approach networking contacts with excitement and conviction, cultivate self-confidence, and practice positive self-talk.

The Advantages of Self-Confidence:

Confidence attracts and spreads. Others are naturally drawn to your energy and passion when you exhibit confidence. This self-assurance opens the door to exciting and memorable interactions, creating an indelible impression on fellow participants, possible mentors, and industry leaders. Remember that believing in oneself is the catalyst for establishing a network success ripple effect.

Self-reflection is essential for good networking. Understanding your networking goals, identifying your skills, embracing your path, and growing self-confidence will set you on a purpose-driven, meaningful, and transformative networking journey. When you enter professional meetings and conferences with self-awareness and a clear sense of direction, every coffee networking break becomes an opportunity to connect authentically, develop genuine relationships, and unlock the doors to unlimited possibilities. Stay loyal to yourself, and let the power of self-reflection and trust in your unique value as a professional guide your networking path.

2.2 Identifying Your Target Network

Finding your ideal network is like charting a course in the vast sea of networking possibilities. Professional networkers stand out because of their ability to identify the contacts most likely to help them achieve their objectives. Let's discuss how to find your way through all the options, how to network effectively, and who to connect with.

Finding the Right People to Ask Questions of

There are always notable participants and leaders at each industry gathering or conference. These people can be an excellent resource for advice, guidance, and possible partnerships. Before going, you should make an effort to learn who they are.

Expert Recommendations on Networking:

"Networking is an essential part of building wealth." U.S. Political Analyst Armstrong Williams- (1)

According to Armstrong Williams, making connections can profoundly affect your career. Your career might take off to new heights if you network with people in positions of power.

Looking for a Shared Passion and Common Interests

Authentic connections are what networking is all about, not just trading business cards. Find other people who share your interests, passions, or aspirations. With these commonalities established, deep discussions are possible.

Words of Wisdom from a Successful Business Owner:

"When networking, focus on building personal relationships rather than professional ones." Entrepreneur and philanthropist Brian E. Boyd Sr.

The words of wisdom from Brian E. Boyd Sr. stress the significance of developing relationships that go beyond mere business ties. By establishing a personal connection and bonding around shared interests, you can strengthen your professional association with one another.

Finding Like-Minded Partners and Friends:

Successful collaborations are often the result of mutual discovery through networking, which is a two-way street. Find other businesses or individuals whose services will enhance your own.

Tips from an Avant-garde Thinker:

"Networking isn't simply about making new acquaintances. It's all about putting people in touch with one another, sharing ideas, and creating new chances. Speaker and pioneer Michele Jennae.

Michele Jennae's recommendations highlight the multifaceted nature of networking. If you approach networking with the mindset of a connector of ideas and possibilities, you can unlock the doors to fruitful partnerships that will further your career.

Taking a Genuine and Considerate Networking Approach:

Networking success hinges on being genuine and treating others with respect when reaching out to new contacts. Strive instead to establish real connections with others and avoid coming across as exploitative.

Insights from a World-Class Executive:

Hunting is not what networking is about. The topic is farming. Relationship building is critical. BNI's Founder and Chairman, Ivan Misner

Ivan Misner's comparison of networking to farming is a brilliant metaphor for the importance of building and maintaining connections in the business world. Building lasting relationships pays off with increased access to resources and social capital.

How to Pinpoint Your Ideal Contacts and Reach Your Goal Network

Finding the right combination of investigation, intuition, and strategic planning will lead you to your desired network. Consider the following to help you zero in on the most promising associations.

- Clarify why you want to network, such as to further your career, find a mentor, or discover new opportunities for collaboration.

- Attendees of a Study: Examining the roster of event participants ahead of time might help you spot key opinion leaders and establish new connections.

- Use social media to your advantage by checking out participants' profiles and networks on LinkedIn to see whether they fit your event's objectives well.

- Seek Out Recommendations From Colleagues Or Mentors: Ask for suggestions from people or groups to help you achieve your networking goals.

- Talk to People: Talk with other attendees at networking events to learn more about their backgrounds and interests.

- Don't just stick to making contacts with people in your field; go out and meet people from other areas of expertise as well.

- The Science and Art of Making an Indelible First Impression

- Keep in mind the value of first impressions while reaching out to new contacts:

- Introduce yourself with assurance, giving out your full name, occupation, and areas of experience.

- Look for shared experiences or hobbies to help you connect with someone on a deeper level than just a professional one.

- Show genuine interest in the thoughts and feelings of other people by listening to them and processing what they have to say.

Sending an appreciation and thank you email or text after a networking meeting is a great way to show appreciation for the time spent talking with the other person.

The actual potential of professional connections can only be unlocked by identifying your target network and conducting networking with sincerity. Successfully navigating the sea of networking opportunities requires a study of essential actors, the pursuit of shared passions, and the recognition of possible collaborators. Keep in mind the guidance of networking gurus and thought leaders as you forge significant connections, and view networking as a tool for both professional development and personal advancement. If you know what you're doing and where you want to go with your networking, you'll be in good shape to enjoy a prosperous future.

2.3 Crafting Your Personal Brand

Personal branding has become increasingly important in today's networking age because it drastically alters one's professional and personal fortunes. Developing a distinct identity may set you apart from the competition and become a leader in your field. Let's investigate personal branding and its many uses, advantages, and critical components that make up a solid and effective brand.

The Science of Influence and the Art of Personal Branding

The term "personal branding" is used to describe the method through which one's professional reputation is cultivated and maintained. You must figure out what you're good at, who you want to work with, and why they should care about you. Your personal brand is the condensed version of your professional life story that you share through numerous means, such as your online profiles, in-person meetings, and public events.

Personal branding's upsides and rewards:

- Your chances of being seen by influential people (like possible employers, mentors, and coworkers) improve when you have a well-developed personal brand.
- You'll be taken more seriously as an expert and leader in your area if you've established a solid personal brand.
- An engaging personal brand makes you stand out and emphasizes individuality in a crowded marketplace.
- Progression in One's Profession Attracting new possibilities and relationships is one way a clearly defined personal brand can help one advance in one's profession.
- A powerful personal brand is a magnet for other successful professionals and prospective customers, significantly boosting your networking efforts.

Well-known branding guidance:

What others say about you while you're not around makes up your "personal brand." CEO and Amazon Co-Founder Jeff Bezos

"Your name is the doorway to your art. You have a mission on Earth; you were put here to make a difference. The question is, "How can you organize your life and career to make this a reality?" Author and Businesswoman Danielle LaPorte

Keys to Establishing Your Own Identity as a Brand:

- Consider your beliefs, interests, and abilities as a starting point for introspection. The basis of a successful personal brand is a compelling "why" and how that motivates your work.

- Define who you want to connect with and impact, whether other individuals or businesses. Make sure the brand's message hits home with them.

- Make an engaging account of your career to date, highlighting your achievements and the contributions you hope to make to your field.

- Brand messaging: Find a way to speak with one voice that reflects your values and expertise everywhere it appears. The messages you send out should be easy to understand and consistent with your brand's history.

- It would be best for your personal brand to be consistent across all channels by developing a unified visual design with a high-quality profile picture, logo, and color palette.

- Create a solid online identity by posting often on social media and maintaining a professional website. Establish trust and authority by providing helpful material and interacting with your target audience.

- Your networking activities should be based on your personal brand. Connect with influential people in your field by participating in industry events, forums, and mentorship programs.

Personal branding examples that succeed:

CEO of Tesla and SpaceX, Elon Musk: Musk's reputation as an entrepreneur hinges on his dedication to improving the world through technological innovation.

Authenticity, empowerment, and a dedication to pulling others up through her media and charity work are central to Oprah Winfrey's personal brand.

Conclusion:

Building a solid personal brand is a life-altering endeavor that can have far-reaching consequences for your professional future. Personal branding may help you stand out in a crowd, build your reputation, and make new connections if you know how to use it effectively. Follow the lead of prominent businesspeople and entrepreneurs by understanding that your reputation is more than a reflection of your abilities; it is also the key to finding your life's work. Authenticity, consistency, and intention are the threads that will hold your personal brand together and propel you toward a powerful and meaningful professional identity. The opportunities available to you through networking are only limited by the strength of your personal brand.

Summary

Congrats on finishing the second chapter of "Network Like a Pro"! This chapter laid the groundwork for successful networking by focusing on self-reflection, finding your target network, and creating your brand. Reminding you of the things to do

- Take a moment to think about what you want to achieve and what you're good at.
- Check out your target network.
- Create your personal brand statement.
- Hey, make sure you update your profiles.
- Make some networking goals.
- Just practice introducing yourself with confidence.
- Get some feedback from mentors or colleagues.
- Chat about industry stuff online.
- Join groups that are specific to your industry.
- Join virtual networking events.

This is a friendly reminder that understanding yourself and your goals is essential for networking. It's the secret sauce to crushing it! Just be yourself, embrace what makes you unique, and have confidence in your skills. Let your true self shine when you're networking.

As you continue, remember that networking isn't about pretending to be someone else but about showing others your actual worth. Just take a second to think about it, figure out your crew, and let your style guide you as you dive deeper into the networking scene. Let's move on to the next chapter - catch you there!

"Introverts can be the best networkers; they just have to find their own style." - Patty Alper

Multiple Choice Questions

1. What is the advantage of having specific networking goals before attending networking events?

a) It allows you to wander aimlessly and meet random people.

b) It helps you approach each interaction with focus and resolve.

c) It guarantees that you will achieve all your networking objectives.

d) It is not essential to have specific goals for networking.

2. According to Armstrong Williams, why is networking essential?

a) Networking can lead to building wealth and fame.

b) Networking can profoundly affect your career and open new opportunities.

c) Networking is a waste of time and effort.

d) Networking is only necessary for people in positions of power.

3. What is the significance of finding people with shared passions and interests in networking?

a) It allows you to trade business cards and make superficial connections.

b) It helps you establish deep discussions and meaningful connections.

c) It is not relevant in networking events.

d) It shows that you are not focused on your networking goals.

4. What does Ivan Misner's metaphor of networking as "farming" imply?

a) Networking is like hunting for new connections aggressively.

b) Building lasting relationships and maintaining connections is essential in networking.

c) Networking is a one-time event without any long-term benefits.

d) Networking should be done with a transactional mindset.

5. What is the term "personal branding" used to describe?

a) The process of creating an impressive LinkedIn profile.

b) The way you present yourself in social gatherings.

c) The method through which one's professional reputation is cultivated and maintained.

d) The act of making connections with influential people.

6. How can a well-developed personal brand benefit your networking efforts?

a) It helps you collect more business cards and connections.

b) It makes you stand out and emphasizes individuality in a crowded marketplace.

c) Personal branding has no impact on networking.

d) It guarantees that you will achieve all your networking objectives.

7. What is the key to establishing a solid personal brand?

a) Posting regularly on social media and having a professional website.

b) Having a high-quality profile picture and logo.

c) Establishing trust and authority through helpful content and interactions.

d) Being authentic, consistent, and intentional in your messaging.

8. What can a well-defined personal brand do for your career?

a) It can make you famous and increase your social media followers.

b) It can help you advance in your profession and attract new opportunities.

c) Personal branding has no impact on career growth.

d) It can guarantee you a high-paying job.

9. How should you approach networking contacts to make a good first impression?

a) Be reserved and avoid sharing personal information.

b) Introduce yourself with confidence, share your name and expertise.

c) Focus only on your own accomplishments and successes.

d) Avoid listening to others and dominate the conversation.

10. What is the role of authenticity, consistency, and intention in personal branding?

a) They are irrelevant and have no impact on personal branding.

b) They are important in building a solid and meaningful professional identity.

c) They can be used to manipulate others in networking.

d) They are not necessary in networking events.

Answers

1. b

2. b

3. b

4. b

5. b, c

6. b

7. d

8. b

9. b

10. b

Chapter 3: Preparing for Successful Networking

Our next stop in "Network Like a Pro" is Chapter 3, "The Ultimate Guide to Successful Networking (at Industry Events)." This chapter discusses the groundwork you should lay for productive networking encounters. We'll show you how to make the most of your time during those little coffee breaks by networking effectively, from gathering information about events to practicing your elevator pitch. Okay, so let's begin!

3.1 Researching Events and Opportunities

Before attending any networking event, it is essential to thoroughly prepare by conducting thorough research. Engaging in pre-event study and planning can significantly enhance your ability to effectively pursue events and opportunities that align with your objectives, interests, and desired professional connections. Please find below a set of valuable steps to assist you in conducting your research:

Establishing Clear Objectives: Engaging in networking activities without a defined purpose may result in overlooking valuable opportunities. Please take a moment to clarify your objectives for networking. Are you interested in finding prospective partners, job opportunities, mentors, or industry insights? Understanding your goals is essential in determining the most suitable events to attend and the most effective networking strategies.

Selecting the Appropriate Events: Given the vast array of events taking place in the media, entertainment, advertising, and production sectors, it is crucial to carefully choose those that are most suitable for your specific skills and professional goals. Please consider exploring conferences and trade shows catering to professionals within your niche. Events that cater to your interests create a community where you can meet individuals with the same mindset and goals and foster meaningful connections.

Please review the attendee list: If available, kindly acquire the list of attendees before the event. I recommend dedicating some time to thoroughly researching and acquainting yourself with the backgrounds and interests of essential individuals with whom you wish to establish connections. Knowing the individuals you want to connect with beforehand can significantly enhance your confidence in networking activities. It also enables you to have more meaningful and productive conversations.

Leverage Social Media: Social media platforms can serve as practical tools to enhance your networking experience even before the commencement of the event. I recommend actively participating in event hashtags and online forums to join in on pre-event discussions. This will let you engage with attendees and contribute to the conversation. Engage with prospective attendees and speakers to formally introduce yourself and convey your genuine excitement about the opportunity to meet them face-to-face. This improves visibility and lets you establish connections before the event's commencement.

Download Event App: In today's digital work ALL conferences and events (even webinars) usually have an associated app. By downloading this you will get access to an incredible amount of data including a delegate list, and in some cases, contact info. This is an invaluable tool to get connected to fellow delegates (and sponsers) ahead of the event and organize meetings.

One well-known saying goes, "By neglecting to prepare adequately, you are essentially setting yourself up for failure." Benjamin Franklin

Entrepreneur's advice: "Always conduct homework before attending networking events. Knowing is indeed empowering, and it can significantly benefit you in understanding the individuals present and their areas of interest. This understanding will provide you with a valuable edge in establishing meaningful connections.- Richard Branson

Please remember that dedicating time and effort to thoroughly researching events and clarifying your objectives will yield positive results, such as meaningful networking opportunities and valuable connections. Proactively equipping yourself for success would be best, significantly distinguishing you from others during coffee networking breaks.

In the upcoming section, we will focus on another crucial element of effective networking: the art of creating your elevator pitch. Your elevator pitch is a concise and impactful summary that effectively communicates your message within a 30-second. Welcome to our platform, where you can create impactful introductions and highlight your distinct value. In Section 3.2, we will delve into the art of crafting a compelling elevator pitch. Let's explore this topic together.

Let's make sure you create an indelible mark on everyone you meet!

3.2 Developing an Elevator Pitch

Envision yourself talking to the individual next to you while waiting for coffee at a business networking event. A natural conversation progression leads them to inquire, "So, what do you do?" Give your presentation in the elevator right now. How should one define and perfect their "elevator pitch"?

You should be able to summarize who you are, what you can do, and the value you bring to the table in less than an elevator ride. An "elevator pitch" is a short business presentation that may be given during an elevator trip, usually no more than 30 seconds.

Here are the components that will set apart your elevator speech:

- Your elevator pitch should begin with a hook, such as a compelling statement or question. This will capture the interest of the audience and get them more involved.
- Advertise what makes you different and unique from everyone else in your field by centering on your USP (Unique Selling Point). Focus on the specifics of your background that prove your competence in the area.
- Personalize Your Pitch. Adjust your pitch based on who you're speaking with and the occasion. Make sure the words and examples you use are relevant to your audience.
- Exhibit the Benefits You Offer: Explain to people what you can do for them. How might your knowledge and experience benefit a potential business partner or employer?
- Infuse your presentation with a genuine interest in your profession and the industry. Sincerity attracts, and others will feel your enthusiasm for your cause.
- Remember that brevity is the key to an elevator pitch, so keep your remarks brief and easy to understand. Maintain clarity and brevity. Don't use any confusing jargon or technical phrases.
- Repeatedly practice your "elevator pitch" until you can deliver it with ease and assurance. If you want to perfect your delivery, try practicing in front of a mirror, with friends, or by recording yourself.

Here's an example of an elevator speech: "Hello, my name is [Your Name], and I'm a digital marketing strategist with a penchant for bridging the gap between brands and their intended consumers. I have led campaigns that increased online awareness and engagement by over 50% for well-known media organizations. I can't wait to investigate potential avenues of cooperation and creativity in the advertising and media sectors.

It's been said that "you never get another chance to make a first impression." Will Rogers

Business Tip: "Your elevator pitch summarizes who you are as a brand in just a few phrases. Make it interesting, unique, and genuine. Delivered with assurance, it can change the way people view you forever. To paraphrase Oprah Winfrey:

Create an engaging elevator pitch to make a solid and lasting impression at business networking events. Remember that networking is about making genuine relationships; your elevator pitch invites you to continue the conversation and connect with others.

Section 3.3 will help you further hone your communication abilities after you've mastered creating a captivating elevator pitch. We'll discuss the best ways to start discussions with strangers, make friends quickly, and make a good impression on everyone you meet. Let us help you look like a seasoned professional at your next networking event.

3.3 Polishing Your Communication Skills

Communication abilities are essential for effective networking. Acquiring the art of connecting with others is necessary to make the most of coffee breaks for networking. Here are some invaluable guidelines and psychological considerations to improve your communication skills:

Active listening requires a genuine interest in what others are saying. Active listening involves giving complete attention, maintaining eye contact, and appropriately nodding or responding to the speaker. Participate in the conversation, ask follow-up questions, and demonstrate appreciation for the other person's insights. Active listening helps you understand the other person better and fosters a more profound connection by making them feel respected and valued.

Conversational authenticity: Be yourself and let your genuine personality shine through. Avoid scripts and memorized phrases. People are drawn to individuals who are secure in their skin because authenticity is magnetic. When true, you build trust and make others comfortable, encouraging them to share more.

Please pay close attention to your body language, as it reveals a great deal about your confidence and transparency. Stand or sit erect, extend a firm handshake, and maintain approachable body language. Crossing your arms can be interpreted as closed off or defensive. Positivity in your body language increases your credibility and communicates that you are approachable. One of my pet peeves is people trying to engage with me and they constantly on their phone, or worse still, eyes daring around the room looking to see who else there is to talk to instead of being present and focused.

The Art of Mirroring: Subtly mirroring the body language and tone of the person you are conversing with can establish rapport and trust. Mirroring demonstrates empathy and can facilitate fellowship. When done naturally and subtly, mirroring can create a strong connection with the other person, making them feel more at ease and understood.

Display empathy for others by comprehending and validating their emotions and experiences. Emotional intelligence is crucial for nurturing meaningful relationships and establishing trust. When you demonstrate empathy, you create a safe space for others to pen up with you and your emotions, resulting in deeper and more genuine conversations.

Understanding the psychology of influence will allow you to communicate more persuasively. Reciprocation (offering assistance or valuable information), social proof (highlighting endorsements or shared experiences), and authority (demonstrating your expertise) are communication techniques that can enhance your impact. Using these psychological stimuli can increase the persuasiveness and memorability of your messages.

Humor and Humility: Humor can break the ice and generate a positive environment. However, use it sparingly and with sensitivity to cultural nuances. Adopt humility by recognizing that you do not know everything and being willing to learn from others. Being humble makes you approachable and relatable, allowing for more genuine connections.

Successful media executive Michelle flourishes in communication by mastering the art of making others feel valued. She actively listens to conversation partners during networking events, asks thoughtful inquiries, and recalls pertinent information regarding their interests. This customized approach leaves a lasting impression and fosters genuine relationships.

Entrepreneurial advice: "Communication is the most essential quality for a leader. It's not just about communicating well; it's about connecting with people authentically and motivating them to act." The billionaire Richard Branson

Communication is a skill that can be continuously developed and honed. Seek feedback from dependable coworkers or mentors, and regularly exercise your communication skills in various settings. Observe effective communicators, attend seminars, and read books on effective communication to continue your development.

By refining your communication skills and integrating psychological effects, you will exude confidence during networking events and cultivate meaningful relationships. Learning the art of communication is the key to networking success, as networking is about establishing genuine relationships.

Section 5 will investigate the world of social media platforms as we continue our networking journey. Utilizing platforms such as LinkedIn can substantially increase your network and opportunities. The following section will explore the digital world of professional connections.

"The currency of real networking is not greed but generosity." - Keith Ferrazzi

Key Pointers

Here are pointers for the homework after Chapter 3

- Look into upcoming networking events.
- Experiment with and improve your elevator pitch.
- Examine and improve your communication and body language.
- Prepare topics for conversation or icebreakers for networking meetings.
- Set a certain amount of new connections that you want to make.

- Make a networking toolkit containing essentials such as business cards and a notepad.
- Seek feedback from a mentor or friend through a fake networking practice session.
- Learn about the keynote speakers and panelists at the events you'll be attending.
- To increase engagement, practice active listening in your regular conversations.
- Consider previous networking experiences and make plans for future encounters.

These tasks will improve your networking abilities and open the road for significant contacts and career advancement! Why not try and write your Elevator Pitch here...

Multiple Choice Questions

1. Why is conducting thorough research before attending a networking event important?

a) It helps you find ways to avoid networking events.

b) It enhances your ability to pursue events that align with your objectives and interests.

c) It saves time by skipping networking events.

d) It allows you to attend any event without specific objectives.

2. How can you benefit from reviewing the attendee list before a networking event?

a) It helps you avoid talking to anyone you don't know.

b) It allows you to be more confident in networking activities.

c) It helps you to ignore the backgrounds and interests of attendees.

d) It makes networking less meaningful.

3. What is the purpose of leveraging social media before a networking event?

a) To avoid engaging with attendees online.

b) To participate in pre-event discussions and engage with attendees.

c) To gather information about events and opportunities.

d) To promote your own brand without connecting with others.

4. An elevator pitch is:

a) A long, detailed presentation about your skills and experiences.

b) A short business presentation given during an elevator ride, usually lasting more than 5 minutes.

c) A concise and impactful summary that communicates your message in less than 30 seconds.

d) A random collection of words and phrases without any specific purpose.

5. What is the first component that sets apart a compelling elevator pitch?

a) Highlighting your background and education.

b) Using complex jargon and technical terms to impress the audience.

c) Starting with a hook, such as a compelling statement or question.

d) Talking about your personal interests and hobbies.

6. Why is conversational authenticity important in an elevator pitch?

a) Authenticity makes your pitch more confusing and less effective.

b) Authenticity makes your pitch seem rehearsed and insincere.

c) People are drawn to individuals who are genuine and secure in their skin.

d) Authenticity is not relevant in networking situations.

7. What is the significance of active listening in networking?

a) It shows others that you are not interested in their thoughts and opinions.

b) It fosters a deeper connection by making others feel respected and valued.

c) It allows you to dominate conversations and talk about yourself.

d) It is not necessary in networking events.

8. How can mirroring body language and tone benefit communication in networking?

a) It can create a sense of confusion and discomfort in the other person.

b) It establishes rapport and trust, making the other person feel at ease and understood.

c) It is considered disrespectful and should be avoided.

d) It is not effective in building connections with others.

9. What are some psychological techniques that can enhance your impact in communication?

a) Reciprocation, social proof, and humility.

b) Interrupting others and using technical jargon.

c) Sarcasm and humor at the expense of others.

d) Dominating conversations and talking about yourself.

10. Why is refining communication skills important for networking success?

a) Networking is about making superficial connections, not genuine relationships.

b) Effective communication allows you to connect with people authentically and motivate them to act.

c) Communication skills are not relevant in networking events.

d) Networking success depends solely on your professional achievements.

Answers

1. b

2. b

3. b

4. c

5. c

6. c

7. b

8. b

9. a

10. b

Chapter 4: Effective Networking Strategies

Chapter 4 of "Network Like a Pro" welcomes you to the definitive guide to networking success (at industry events). Learn how to better your networking and make more meaningful contacts using the information provided in this chapter. We'll go through everything from active listening to building genuine connections as ways to set yourself apart at your next networking event.

"Success in networking comes from sincere, meaningful connections, not from a transactional approach." - Harvey Mackay

4.1 Active Listening and Genuine Engagement

In the realm of networking, the practice of active listening can significantly influence one's capacity to establish enduring connections. Effective communication extends beyond simply listening to the words being spoken. It entails actively engaging in the present moment, demonstrating authentic curiosity, and comprehending the other person's point of view. Let us explore the concept of active listening and its potential to enhance your networking skills.

The Significance of Being Present:

Active listening is a practice that demonstrates to the individual with whom you are interacting that they have your complete and undivided attention. Showing active engagement in the conversation conveys a strong message of appreciation for the individual and their ideas. It fosters a perception of reverence and engenders a sense of significance and validation in the other individual.

Strategies for Excelling in Active Listening

Please ensure that you maintain your complete focus: During a bustling networking event, it may be tempting to divert your attention by scanning the surroundings or using your mobile device. Nevertheless, it is essential to exert deliberate effort to direct your attention exclusively toward the individual you are conversing with.

Maintain eye contact as it demonstrates sincerity and fosters a sense of connection. It presents a sincere interest in the speaker's words and conveys undivided attention on your part.

It is advisable to refrain from interrupting or rushing when engaging in conversation. Allowing the individual to fully express their thoughts before responding is essential. The act of interrupting can be viewed as dismissive and potentially impede the natural flow of a conversation.

Engage in the practice of empathetic listening by making an effort to comprehend and acknowledge the emotions, needs, and concerns of others. Please consider adopting a perspective of empathy and responding in a manner that fosters a stronger connection with the individual.

The Psychological Effects of Active Listening

Active listening improves the quality of your interactions and has a significant psychological impact on both parties involved. Active listening plays a prominent role in fostering trust and establishing meaningful connections.

Establishing Trust: By actively listening, you effectively convey trustworthiness and dependability. Trust is the fundamental basis for establishing and maintaining relationships, and engaging in active listening is a tangible demonstration of your reliability and approachability for others to confide in.

Validating Emotions: By providing the other person with your complete attention, you acknowledge and validate their emotions and experiences. This validation promotes an atmosphere of inclusivity and shared comprehension.

Enhancing Rapport: Active listening fosters an environment conducive to open and sincere communication. It is essential to build rapport and foster a conducive environment where individuals feel comfortable expressing their thoughts and ideas.

Examples from real-life situations

The Significance of Active Listening at a Media Summit: At a media summit, a marketing executive demonstrated the power of attentive listening by engaging with a young entrepreneur who faced challenges in increasing the visibility of her startup. The executive showed empathy towards her challenges and provided valuable advice, resulting in a collaborative effort that proved mutually beneficial.

During an industry event, a public relations professional demonstrated empathetic listening skills by attentively engaging with a colleague facing work-related stress. The sincere support and empathy provided by the colleague contributed to a sense of value and nurtured a robust professional relationship.

Advice for Entrepreneurs:

Active listening is a captivating and enigmatic phenomenon, possessing a transformative power. The individuals who lend us their ears and attentively listen to our thoughts and feelings are the ones we naturally gravitate towards. When we are actively engaged in being listened to, it has the profound effect of shaping our identity, allowing us to develop and grow.

Developing proficiency in active listening can distinguish you from others in networking events. You can establish a lasting positive impression by demonstrating the ability to make others feel valued and understood. The following section will delve into creating a lasting impact by developing a remarkable elevator pitch.

4.2 Making a Memorable First Impression

First reactions serve as stepping stones for deeper interactions. They influence how people see us and have the power to make or shatter possibilities. Mastering the art of leaving a lasting first impression is crucial in the fast-paced networking world. We'll discuss the importance of first impressions, how to make an impression that counts, and the potent psychological phenomenon known as the "Halo Effect."

The Value of First Impressions

According to research, it just takes a few seconds for someone to create their first opinion of another individual. This means that the initial few seconds of a networking event might be crucial for building rapport and leaving a lasting impression.

Techniques to Make a Positive Impact

Dress for Success: First impressions are greatly influenced by your appearance. As you dress for the occasion, be professional while keeping in mind the norms and culture of your sector.

The Key Is Confidence: Through your posture, body language, and a solid handshake, exude confidence. People are more likely to interact with you when you are confident since it shows you are competent. Own it!

Warm, sincere smiles: A genuine grin has the power to transform. It not only humanizes you, but it also exudes positivity and warmth.

Be Aware: Take an active interest in the conversations, viewpoints, and ideas of others. Do not look at your phone or wander around, which can indicate boredom.

Create a captivating elevator pitch introducing you, your experience, and what you can contribute to the conversation. Make it specific to the occasion and the people you are speaking with.

Networking's "Halo Effect"

The halo effect makes one's opinion of someone as a whole affects how they are perceived regarding particular qualities or skills. People are more inclined to infer positive traits about a person from their first impression, even if they haven't been directly observed.

Advantages of Creating a Good First Impression

Building rapport and trust: An excellent first impression builds trust, encouraging people to consider you a prospective partner or collaborator.

Increased Likability: Positive impression-makers are attracted to others naturally. This likeability can result in more profound, more lasting bonds.

Opportunities: Making a good first impression enhances your chances of being contacted about potential partnerships, initiatives, or employment opportunities.

Real-World Case

A creative director met a young graphic designer at an advertising conference. The designer made an excellent first impression with his friendly grin, self-assurance, and polished elevator pitch. Later, the creative director contacted me to work with me on a project, which resulted in a fruitful collaboration.

Advice for Entrepreneurs:

"A first impression is something you never get a second chance to make." (Will Rogers)

You can up your networking game by grasping the value of first impressions and utilizing the Halo Effect. Making a good impression initially paves the way for worthwhile interactions and successful relationships. In the coming chapters, we'll explore the art of developing genuine connections using efficient networking techniques.

4.3 Nurturing Authentic Relationships

In the field of networking, cultivating genuine relationships is of utmost importance. To establish enduring influence and facilitate meaningful connections, it is necessary to possess a comprehensive understanding of the psychology underlying human interactions. One can achieve this objective by strategically employing psychological techniques to bolster rapport-building. In the following chapter, we will explore the practice of cultivating genuine relationships through psychological strategies. Additionally, we will examine the utilization of psychological techniques to create a positive impact on others.

The Significance of Empathy

Empathy serves as the fundamental basis for establishing meaningful connections. By adopting a perspective of empathy and acknowledging the emotions of others, one can cultivate an authentic relationship that surpasses mere surface-level networking. Demonstrating empathy enables individuals to experience a sense of being recognized, esteemed, and comprehended.

Developing Empathy

Enhancing Listening Skills: Expand your listening skills by incorporating emotional mirroring and employing validating statements. Demonstrate sincere concern for the emotions of the individual in question.

Body Language: Observing non-verbal cues such as facial expressions and gestures is essential to understand underlying emotions better.

The principle of reciprocity

Reciprocity is a significant psychological phenomenon in which individuals experience a solid inclination to reciprocate acts of kindness or favors. By exhibiting generosity and offering assistance, individuals can foster a sense of obligation in others, thereby increasing the likelihood of receiving reciprocal actions.

Leveraging the Potential of Reciprocity

Prioritize Value Provision: Take the initiative to offer others your assistance, insights, or resources without anticipating immediate reciprocation.

Establishing Trust: By consistently demonstrating trustworthiness and dependability, individuals are more likely to trust you, fostering mutually advantageous relationships.

The halo effect is a cognitive bias involving the inclination to attribute multiple positive qualities to individuals based on a favorable trait or initial impression. An excellent initial image can make others perceive you as highly competent, amiable, and reliable.

Developing a Favorable Halo Effect

Exude Confidence and Warmth: It is advisable to present oneself with a combination of confidence and warmth, as these attributes have the potential to create a positive halo effect, thereby enhancing the perception others have of you.

Dressing professionally and appropriately for any given occasion can have a favorable and enduring effect on individuals.

Psychological Manipulation Techniques

Networking should ideally be founded on authentic connections. However, having a grasp of specific psychological principles can enhance your ability to establish rapport more efficiently:

The concept of mirroring: Employ the technique of subtly replicating the body language and speech patterns of the individual with whom you are interacting. The practice of mirroring can facilitate the development of familiarity and comfort.

The Principle of Reciprocity suggests that when commencing a conversation, it is advisable to begin by offering a small favor or compliment. This principle of reciprocity is activated, thereby increasing the likelihood of the other individual responding positively.

An Account Based on Real Events

During a media conference, an up-and-coming marketer effectively applied the reciprocity principle by imparting valuable industry insights to a seasoned executive. This modest display of generosity initiated a mentorship opportunity, resulting in a mutually advantageous relationship that facilitated the marketer's professional advancement.

The Significance of Establishing Connections:

Empathy is taking on another person's perspective, hearing what they are hearing, and feeling what they are feeling.

By comprehending the psychological intricacies of networking, one can cultivate significant connections and establish a favorable and enduring impression in the minds of others. These psychological techniques can enhance networking achievements and facilitate access to unforeseen opportunities. As we progress in our exploration of networking, let us delve into the realm of online platforms and examine how they can be harnessed to extend your network beyond the confines of physical events.

"Trust is the glue of life. It's the most essential ingredient in effective communication. It's the foundational principle that holds all relationships." - Stephen Covey

Summary

In Chapter 4, we looked at some fantastic networking tactics. What is extremely important? Listening intently! Yes, connecting with others means genuinely hearing what they say and feeling their vibrations. And believe me when I say that making a great first impression is a game changer. Those first few moments may shape the entire conversation, so here are some pointers to help you leave a lasting impression.

But hold on; there's more! Developing genuine relationships is the ultimate networking trick. It's not about accumulating contacts like trading cards; it's about making real connections that will last.

With these methods, you're ready to take on the networking environment with confidence and flair. Remember that it's not just about who you meet but also about how you form meaningful relationships. We'll continue to press forward and uncover many more professional networking ideas together! You've got this.

Multiple Choice Questions

1. Active listening in networking involves:

a) Merely hearing the words being spoken.

b) Engaging in the present moment and showing authentic curiosity.

c) Speaking more than listening.

d) Checking your mobile device during conversations

2. Why is maintaining eye contact important in active listening?

a) It shows you are not interested in the conversation.

b) It conveys sincerity and fosters a sense of connection.

c) It helps you avoid distractions.

d) It allows you to interrupt the speaker.

3. What is one of the strategies for excelling in active listening?

a) Interrupting the speaker to share your thoughts.

b) Rushing to respond without fully understanding the other person's point of view.

c) Maintaining complete focus and attention on the individual you are conversing with.

d) Avoiding eye contact to avoid appearing too assertive.

4. The psychological effects of active listening include:

a) Establishing trust, validating emotions, and enhancing rapport.

b) Dismissing the other person's thoughts and ideas.

c) Ignoring the emotions and concerns of others.

d) Making others feel undervalued and misunderstood

5. Making a memorable first impression at networking events involves:

a) Dressing casually and informally.

b) Avoiding eye contact to appear more mysterious.

c) Exuding confidence through posture and body language.

d) Using your phone during conversations to appear busy.

6. The "Halo Effect" in networking refers to:

a) The psychological phenomenon where a first impression influences how specific qualities are perceived.

b) The negative impact of making a good first impression.

c) The strategy of dressing professionally to create a positive impact on others.

d) The act of interrupting others during conversations.

7. How can empathy contribute to genuine relationships in networking?

a) By ignoring the emotions of others.

b) By demonstrating a lack of interest in others' perspectives.

c) By acknowledging and validating the emotions of others.

d) By avoiding eye contact and mirroring body language.

8. The principle of reciprocity suggests that:

a) Offering assistance and showing generosity can create a sense of obligation in others.

b) Networking should only be based on authentic connections.

c) Interrupting others during conversations is acceptable.

d) Dressing professionally has no impact on first impressions.

9. The networking technique of mirroring involves:

a) Replicating the body language and speech patterns of others.

b) Ignoring the emotions and needs of others.

c) Avoiding eye contact during conversations.

d) Interrupting others to make your point.

10. What is the significance of establishing connections in networking?

a) It allows you to manipulate others using psychological techniques.

b) It fosters trust and enduring impressions.
c) It hinders your ability to grow professionally.

d) It encourages selfish behaviors and disregards the needs of others.

Answers

1. b

2. b

3. c

4. a

5. c

6. a

7. c

8. a

9. a

10. b

Chapter 5: Leveraging Online Networking Platforms

In the era of digital advancements, online networking platforms have emerged as essential tools for professionals aiming to enhance their network and explore potential career prospects. LinkedIn is widely regarded as the primary platform for establishing and cultivating your digital professional identity among these platforms. In the following chapter, I will guide how to utilize LinkedIn and other online platforms effectively to optimize your networking abilities and establish enduring professional connections.

"The single biggest problem in communication is the illusion that it has taken place." - George Bernard Shaw

5.1 LinkedIn Your Digital Professional Identity

LinkedIn, commonly known as the "Facebook for professionals," is a social media platform that prioritizes cultivating significant connections within the business community. In contrast to other social media platforms that primarily facilitate informal interactions, LinkedIn functions as a virtual sanctuary for professionals, businesses, and individuals seeking employment opportunities. As a result, it has become a preferred platform for purposeful networking.

The Advantages of LinkedIn: A Revolutionary Tool for Professionals

The influence of LinkedIn on professionals across diverse industries is indisputable. Allow me to elucidate why this development is considered a significant breakthrough.

Global Reach: LinkedIn offers the opportunity to connect with professionals from diverse locations across the globe, surpassing geographical limitations. Engaging in global outreach initiatives provides a valuable opportunity to significantly expand your professional network and expose yourself to diverse perspectives and potential opportunities.

Targeted Networking: Unlike conventional networking events, which can present difficulties in identifying relevant connections, LinkedIn offers a platform for precise targeting. It is possible to readily identify and establish contact with individuals within your industry who share similar interests or are employed by your desired companies.

Brand Building: LinkedIn provides users with the tools and resources necessary to effectively establish and cultivate a personal brand, making the process of brand building more accessible and efficient than ever before. Using your profile, you can effectively demonstrate your skills, achievements, and expertise, constructing a compelling narrative that draws in suitable opportunities.

Developing Your LinkedIn Profile: Establishing Your Online Identity

Your LinkedIn profile is your digital representation and is essential to make it attractive and compelling. Let us delve into the process of crafting an exceptional profile:

Headline: Craft an impactful headline that effectively conveys your professional role, expertise, and distinctive strengths. Please ensure that your work demonstrates creativity while also maintaining clarity and conciseness.

Summary and Background: This section will provide a concise overview. This section serves as your elevator pitch. Please utilize this section to present your professional narrative, emphasize your accomplishments, and articulate your career objectives.

Experience and Skills: Present your professional background, emphasizing your achievements and areas of proficiency. Including endorsements and recommendations from colleagues and clients enhance the credibility of one's professional profile.

Establishing and Expanding Your Professional Network

The value of LinkedIn resides in the connections you establish and their ability to enhance your network and impact. Here are several strategies for establishing meaningful connections:

Strategic Connections: Exercise discernment when initiating connection requests. Customize each request, referencing shared interests or mutual acquaintances to build a connection.

Create and distribute compelling and insightful content consistently. Creating effective posts not only attracts new connections but also helps maintain the interest of your current network.

LinkedIn Groups: It is advisable to consider joining groups pertinent to your industry and personal interests. Participate in substantive discussions, demonstrate your expertise, and establish new professional relationships.

Gaining Insight into the LinkedIn Algorithm

LinkedIn's algorithm determines the visibility of your content. Recognizing its potential to enhance your reach and engagement:

The level of engagement plays a significant role: Posts that receive a higher number of likes, comments, and shares are considered more valuable, resulting in increased visibility.

Maintaining Consistency: Posting engaging content regularly will indicate to the algorithm that you are an active and valuable participant within the community.

Case Studies: Transforming Lives through Individual Connections

The profound impact of LinkedIn has significantly influenced numerous professionals, fundamentally changing the course of their careers. Please find below a compilation of success stories:

Transitioning from Job Seeker to Dream Job: Through diligent efforts, a committed individual engaged in strategic networking on LinkedIn's professional platform, establishing a direct connection with the Human Resources Manager of a prominent company. As a result of this proactive approach, they successfully secured their long-awaited dream job in their desired position.

Growing Business Horizons: A freelance graphic designer effectively utilized LinkedIn as a platform to showcase their professional portfolio, resulting in valuable collaborations with esteemed clients and a significant increase in business opportunities.

Remember, LinkedIn is all about networking and give and take. Comment and engage with the creators and people you want to get linked with or noticed by them. Follow the creators and look into their posts to see how to grow their connections and build their personal brands to get recognized by industry professionals.

Embrace the Competitive Edge of LinkedIn. LinkedIn is a precious platform for professionals looking to broaden their professional network, establish meaningful relationships, and cultivate a strong personal brand that can lead to numerous opportunities.

1. LinkedIn Enhancing Your Professional Journey

LinkedIn is more than a mere social media platform. It serves as a virtual ecosystem that has the potential to impact your professional trajectory significantly. Let us delve into several fundamental aspects of how LinkedIn can dramatically affect your professional endeavors:

2. Establishing a Personal Brand with Ease

LinkedIn offers a robust platform enabling individuals to demonstrate their skills, achievements, and expertise effectively. By implementing profile optimization techniques, individuals can establish a powerful personal brand that effectively connects with their intended audience and distinguishes them from their competitors.

3. A Fresh Approach to Career Advancement

LinkedIn can significantly impact your career progression if you seek employment, work as a freelancer, or manage your agency.

Utilizing Job Search Filters: LinkedIn's advanced search filters enable users to effectively identify suitable job opportunities by refining search criteria such as location, industry, and experience level.

Customizing Applications: By leveraging insights from company pages and connections, individuals can tailor their applications to specific employers, enhancing their interview prospects.

Attention all freelancers and agency owners:

Demonstrating Your Portfolio: The media upload feature on LinkedIn enables you to exhibit your professional work, providing prospective clients with a visual depiction of your expertise.

Establishing Credibility: Leveraging recommendations and endorsements can effectively cultivate trust and establish a strong reputation within their respective industry.

4. Establishing Meaningful Connections

LinkedIn's core strength is facilitating connections with professionals with similar interests, influential figures within various industries, and prospective clients or partners.

Tips for Effective Networking:

Customized Invitations: Create tailored connection requests that demonstrate a sincere interest in the recipient and shared interests.

Participate in relevant LinkedIn groups to engage with professionals who share your passions and hobbies.

5. Gaining Insight into the LinkedIn Algorithm

The algorithm employed by LinkedIn is crucial in determining the level of visibility your content receives. Gaining a comprehensive understanding of the mechanics behind this process can significantly enhance your ability to optimize your online presence and increase the likelihood of your posts achieving viral status.

Tips for Algorithm Development:

The Value of Engagement: The algorithm prioritizes content that garners engagement in likes, comments, and shares. Promote active participation by creating content that stimulates critical thinking and captivates the audience through compelling narratives.

Consider the timing of your posts to optimize visibility and engagement among your target audience. Posting when they are most active can significantly enhance the likelihood of your content being noticed.

6. Transforming Your Life Within Weeks

The transformative potential of LinkedIn extends beyond the mere expansion of one's professional network, as it also serves as a gateway to new and promising opportunities. By actively engaging and participating while leveraging the tools provided by the platform, you can observe substantial improvements in your professional life within a few weeks.

Harness the potential of online networking and allow LinkedIn to serve as the driving force that transforms your networking endeavors.

5.2 Building a Strong Online Presence

A prominent online presence is no longer a choice in the digital age but a necessity. As we delve deeper into online networking, let's examine how you can leverage various platforms, particularly LinkedIn, to develop a remarkable personal brand and establish a robust online presence that attracts opportunities and demonstrates your expertise.

The Influence of Personal Branding

Your personal brand is your distinctive professional identity. It distinguishes you from the competition and leaves an indelible mark on your network. How to develop an intriguing personal brand:

- First and foremost, be authentic and genuine to yourself. Transparency resonates with others and facilitates trust building.
- Determine your niche by identifying your strengths and areas of expertise. Concentrating on a niche will enable you to become an authority in your chosen field.
- Consistency Is Crucial: Keep your online persona consistent across platforms. Use the same professional headshot, hues, and tone of voice for all communications.
- Displaying Your Knowledge on LinkedIn. LinkedIn provides a multitude of instruments for effectively showcasing your expertise. Here's how to maximize their use:
- Share thought leadership articles on topics pertinent to your industry on LinkedIn Articles. Share your essential insights, experiences, and knowledge.
- Regularly engage with the content of others by liking, commenting, and sharing. Engaging thoughtfully allows you to develop a network of followers.
- Create and distribute brief videos discussing industry trends, offering advice, and sharing success stories. Videos are captivating and compelling to make an impression.

Establishing Professional Connections

The expansion of one's network is essential for obtaining exposure and opportunities. Here are some strategies to effectively expand your network:

Connect with Intention: Personalize your message when sending connection requests. Explain why you would like to connect and how you can both benefit.

Utilize Alumni and Events: Participate in LinkedIn alum groups and network with other graduates. Attend virtual industry events and network with attendees afterward.

Real-World Illustrations of Remarkable Online Presence

Numerous influential entrepreneurs have mastered the art of creating a remarkable online presence. Let's examine a few instances:

Example 1: John, the Master of Digital Marketing

John shares marketing insights and strategies frequently on LinkedIn. His captivating articles and videos have established him as an authority in his profession. His online presence has attracted prominent clients and opportunities to speak at industry events.

Sarah, the Leadership Coach, is Example 2.

Sarah's LinkedIn profile contains compelling endorsements from clients whose lives have been transformed under her guidance. Her genuineness and consistent participation have made her a highly sought-after leadership coach with a flourishing online community.

Leveraging LinkedIn's Power for Entrepreneurs

Entrepreneurs can use LinkedIn to promote their ventures and establish a solid online presence:

Create a company page to highlight your organization's mission and accomplishments.

Thought leadership: As an entrepreneur, discuss your industry's challenges and innovative solutions.

Networking Opportunities: Participate in LinkedIn groups and events to connect with other entrepreneurs, potential partners, and investors.

The Effects of Online Presence

A powerful online presence can do marvels for your business and career:

An exceptional online presence increases your exposure to a global audience.

Consistent collaboration and thought leadership establishes you as a trustworthy authority.

Your online presence attracts opportunities, partnerships, and even employment offers.

Accept the Digital Universe

A solid online presence is your ticket to success in today's interconnected world. It is the key to uncovering possibilities and establishing yourself as an industry thought leader.

By recognizing the power of personal branding and utilizing LinkedIn, you can establish an outstanding online presence that distinguishes you from the competition. The journey towards perfecting networking etiquette continues as we explore the art of small talk, building enduring relationships, and confidently navigating networking events.

5.3 Engaging in Virtual Networking Opportunities

In the constantly changing networking landscape, virtual platforms have become a game-changer. Embracing virtual networking can provide access to many opportunities and connections, enabling you to extend your reach beyond physical boundaries. This chapter will discuss the benefits of virtual networking and how to locate and engage in virtual networking opportunities effectively.

The Benefits of Virtual Networking

Virtual networking provides several benefits that complement traditional face-to-face interactions:

- Connect with professionals from around the globe from the comfort of your home or office.
- Participate in networking opportunities and events at your convenience to accommodate hectic schedules.
- Virtual networking typically requires a small financial outlay, making it accessible to everyone.

Utilizing Virtual Networking Platforms

As stated previously, LinkedIn is an effective instrument for virtual networking. Here are some additional venues where you can engage in active virtual networking:

- Join industry-specific online forums and communities where professionals congregate to discuss trends, share knowledge, and seek advice.
- Attend webinars and virtual conferences hosted by influencers in your industry. Participate in live question-and-answer sessions and converse with other attendees.
- Platforms like Facebook and Reddit host industry-specific groups where professionals collaborate and network.

Guidelines for Efficient Virtual Networking

To leave a lasting impression in a virtual environment requires some finesse. Use these suggestions to stand out:

- Optimize Your Online Profiles: Ensure that your LinkedIn and other social media profiles are up-to-date and that they highlight your expertise and achievements.
- Participate in Online Discussions: Leave insightful comments on posts related to your industry and share your thoughts. Engaging with the content of others helps to establish connections.
- Utilize Video Calls: When applicable, propose video calls to facilitate a more personalized interaction. Eye contact and facial expressions strengthen the bond between people.

Webinars and virtual networking events

Virtual networking events and webinars provide one-of-a-kind opportunities to connect with peers and industry executives. Here's how to locate and capitalize on such occasions:

- Virtual networking events and webinars are listed on websites such as Eventbrite and Meetup. Search for industry- and interest-related events.
- Numerous associations and organizations in the industry conduct virtual events for their members. Join pertinent organizations and maintain awareness of their networking opportunities.

Establishing Connections in a Virtual Environment

Combining empathy and proactive engagement is necessary to establish genuine virtual relationships.

Even in virtual interactions, attentive listening remains essential. Display genuine curiosity in the opinions of others.

After virtual networking events, you should follow up with the individuals you are connected with. Send personalized messages expressing your desire to maintain communication.

The Future of Networking: Accepting the Virtual Transition

As the world embraces digital transformation, virtual networking has become vital for professionals to connect, learn, and develop. Embrace virtual networking opportunities, and you will discover new horizons and expand your network.

Virtual networking is an indispensable talent for contemporary professionals. You will thrive in the ever-changing networking world by participating actively in virtual networking platforms, attending seminars and events, and cultivating meaningful relationships. As we progress, we will discuss mastering networking etiquette, perfecting the art of small conversation, and following up with potential connections to foster long-lasting relationships.

"Effective communication is 20% what you know and 80% how you feel about what you know." - Jim Rohn

Things to do now after this chapter

Networking champ! After exploiting online platforms, let's improve your networking game. Fun and rewarding homework tasks to do after this chapter for you are

- Refresh Your LinkedIn Profile: Add a catchy title, compelling summary, and professional photo. Let's shine online!
- Connect and Engage: LinkedIn at least three new industry contacts. Personalize and start meaningful interactions.
- Share Your Expertise: Write a thought-provoking LinkedIn post or article. Share helpful advice to spark conversation.

- Join Relevant Communities: Look for industry-related LinkedIn communities. Participate in conversations of a few that resonate. Learn and teach.
- Clean Up Your Digital Presence: Google your name to see what appears. Change privacy settings or content if it's questionable.
- Influencers & Industry Leaders: Follow LinkedIn updates from industry leaders and influencers. Like, comment, or share their posts.
- Attend virtual networking events or webinars. Practice virtual interaction and find new friends.

Online networking can be just as excellent and beneficial as in-person networking. Give these things your best to enhance your web presence and network quickly. Enjoy networking!

Multiple Choice Questions

1. LinkedIn is often referred to as the "Facebook for professionals" because:

a) It focuses on informal interactions and socializing.

b) It prioritizes cultivating significant connections within the business community.

c) It is primarily used for sharing personal updates and photos.

d) It limits networking opportunities to specific industries.

2. What is one advantage of using LinkedIn for networking?

a) It only allows connections with people in your local area.

b) It provides limited opportunities for brand building.

c) It enables global reach, connecting with professionals from diverse locations.

d) It is a platform for casual interactions and socializing.

3. How can LinkedIn help in developing a personal brand?

a) By limiting the amount of information you can share on your profile.

b) By offering advanced search filters for job seekers.

c) By providing tools and resources to effectively demonstrate skills and achievements.

d) By focusing solely on the connection with current colleagues.

4. To make a LinkedIn profile compelling, one should:

a) Avoid using a professional headshot to maintain privacy.

b) Create a headline that does not effectively convey professional expertise.

c) Present achievements and expertise in the experience and skills sections.

d) Omit any endorsements or recommendations from colleagues.

5. How can you expand your professional network effectively on LinkedIn?

a) Send generic connection requests to as many people as possible.

b) Participate in LinkedIn groups related to your industry and interests.

c) Avoid engaging with the content of others to maintain privacy.

d) Only connect with people in your immediate local area.

6. What is one benefit of virtual networking platforms, like LinkedIn, compared to face-to-face interactions?

a) They are more time-consuming and costly.

b) They limit networking opportunities to specific industries.

c) They provide access to a global audience from the comfort of your location.

d) They are less effective in establishing meaningful connections.

7. How can you optimize your online presence for networking purposes?

a) By having an incomplete and outdated LinkedIn profile.

b) By engaging with the content of others through likes, comments, and shares.

c) By avoiding video calls and sticking to text-based communication.

d) By using different profile photos and information on various social media platforms.

8. How can attending virtual networking events and webinars benefit professionals?

a) They provide opportunities to meet only local professionals.

b) They offer a chance to engage in informal socializing.

c) They allow for precise targeting of potential connections.

d) They enable connection with peers and industry executives from diverse locations.

9. What is one way to establish genuine connections in a virtual networking environment?

a) By avoiding personalization and sending generic messages to all connections.

b) By participating actively in online discussions and showing curiosity in others' opinions.

c) By limiting interactions to text-based communication only.

d) By avoiding follow-up messages after virtual networking events.

10. Why is virtual networking considered a game-changer in the networking landscape?

a) It is more time-consuming and costly than face-to-face networking.

b) It provides limited opportunities for global connections.

c) It offers access to opportunities beyond physical boundaries and accommodates busy schedules.

d) It restricts networking to specific industries.

Answers

1. b

2. c

3. c

4. c

5. b

6. c

7. b

8. d

9. b

10. c

Chapter 6: Networking Etiquette and Best Practices

Greetings and welcome to Chapter 6 of "Network Like a Pro: Guide to Successful Networking at Industry Events." In the following chapter, we will examine the principles of networking etiquette and explore the most effective strategies for establishing genuine and impactful connections with others. Our approach prioritizes cultivating meaningful human-to-human interactions, establishing genuine relationships rather than solely seeking transactional benefits.

"Success is to be measured not so much by the position that one has reached in life as by the obstacles which he has overcome." - Booker T. Washington

6.1 Approaching Strangers with Confidence

It can be nerve-wracking to approach strangers at networking events, but with the right attitude, you can generate confidence and effortlessly form positive connections. This section will discuss practical ways to help you appear more confident, engage people effectively, form lasting friendships, and leave others with a favorable impression.

- Cultivate Your Self-Confidence: Confidence is an alluring attribute that can significantly alter how others view you. To cultivate self-confidence:
- Substitute self-doubt with positive affirmations by using positive self-talk. Recall your strengths and the value you contribute to conversations.

- Set Obvious Intentions: Before attending a networking event, you should establish clear goals for what you expect to accomplish. Focus on fostering genuine relationships rather than pursuing immediate gains.

- Recognize that each individual has distinctive qualities to offer. Accept yourself as you are, and do not need to appear to be someone else.

- Engage and Attend with Purpose: When you handle networking with a genuine interest in others and an eagerness to engage with purpose, you'll naturally attract people and create meaningful connections.

- Active listening involves being utterly present during conversations. Give the speaker your undivided attention, bow, smile, and respond thoughtfully to their remarks.

- Find a middle ground: Create a sense of camaraderie by identifying shared interests or experiences. This can include anything from pastimes and travel experiences to preferred literature and films.

Your body language has a significant impact on how approachable you appear. Maintain an open stance, make direct eye contact, and avoid crossing your arms, which can indicate defensiveness.

The Science of Making Friends and Connections: Developing friendships through networking entails establishing genuine relationships with individuals that go beyond superficial exchanges. This is how:

- Be Sincere in Your Approach: Instead of approaching conversations with an agenda, demonstrate a genuine interest in the other person and what they say.

- Be a Good Listener: Individuals value being heard. Exhibit empathetic behavior, ask additional inquiries, and demonstrate that you respect their viewpoint.

- Be Vulnerable: Authentic relationships frequently require a degree of vulnerability. Share pertinent experiences or tales that demonstrate your humanity.
- Mastering First Impressions: First impressions are influential and can determine the trajectory of your networking interactions. Consider the following suggestions to make an impact:
- When meeting someone for the first time, you should offer a firm handshake and keep eye contact. It communicates assurance and sincerity.
- A genuine smile easily creates a favorable impression. It places others at ease and invites them to interact with you immediately.
- Craft a compelling and concise elevator speech that highlights your expertise and passion. Practice it until it becomes second nature.
- Positive Body Language: Exhibiting positive body language indicates receptivity and interest. Maintain an upright posture and use open gestures.

Utilize Psychological Techniques: Employ psychological techniques to influence others and build stronger relationships positively:

- Mirroring: Subtly mirror the body language and cadence of the person you are conversing with. This can foster a sense of rapport and familiarity.
- Complimenting others: Offer genuine compliments that emphasize the individual's accomplishments or distinctive qualities.
- Positively frame your sentences and emphasize solutions rather than challenges when using active language. Positive language can elevate a conversation's mood.
- Calling people by their names: When meeting a new person, repeat their name several times throughout the

conversation. It demonstrates that you respect and remember them.

Combining self-assurance, genuine engagement, and a positive mentality makes establishing long-lasting relationships with others at networking events possible. Adopt a human-to-human approach, and you'll find that people will naturally gravitate toward you, opening doors to thrilling opportunities and meaningful relationships. Remember that networking is about creating a supportive community; by supporting others, you create a network that also cares for you.

6.2 Mastering the Art of Small Talk

Engaging in casual conversation is a crucial starting point for establishing significant connections during networking events. Although it may appear superficial upon initial observation, mastering this tool can profoundly impact how others perceive us. In this section, we will further examine the practice of small talk and provide valuable insights on engaging individuals effectively, making a lasting impression, and cultivating meaningful connections through seemingly informal conversations.

The Importance of Small Talk: Despite its focus on ordinary subjects, small talk is crucial in building rapport and fostering a relaxed environment for more meaningful connections. By acquiring proficiency in engaging in casual conversation, one can:

Breaking the ice: Initiating Conversation: Engaging in small talk establishes rapport, alleviates initial apprehension, and facilitates the transition into more meaningful conversations.

Discovering Common Ground: By engaging in informal discussions, it is possible to identify mutual interests, experiences, or values that serve as the foundation for establishing more profound connections.

Display Authentic Interest: Participating in casual conversation showcases your genuine curiosity and empathy, creating a sense of worth and acknowledgment for others.

Tips for Engaging in Small Talk: Engaging in small talk can be a seamless and pleasant experience by following these practical tips:

- Practice being fully present and attentive during conversations by giving your undivided attention to the individual you are engaging with. Minimize potential distractions, such as refraining from checking your mobile device or engaging in visual scanning of the surroundings.
- Please take advantage of Open-Ended Inquiries: Rather than posing questions that elicit simple yes or no responses, employ open-ended queries that prompt the individual to provide more extensive information about their experiences or perspectives.
- Join in active listening. It is essential to actively focus on the speaker's verbal and non-verbal communication signals. Demonstrate engagement by utilizing verbal affirmations and non-verbal cues such as nods.
- Please provide narratives or personal experiences relevant to the current topic of discussion. Anecdotes from individuals can cultivate a heightened level of interpersonal bonding.
- Creating a Memorable Impact: To effectively leave a favorable impression on individuals through casual conversation:
- Maintain a positive and enthusiastic demeanor when engaging in small talk, displaying genuine enthusiasm and a

positive attitude. Positivity is highly contagious and has a magnetic effect on others.

- Utilize humor Strategically: Suitably employing humor can effectively alleviate tension and foster a comfortable environment. It is essential to exercise caution and awareness regarding cultural sensitivities, and it is advisable to refrain from making offensive jokes.

- Demonstrate Empathy and Compassion: Recognize and affirm the emotions and experiences of the individual. The cultivation of empathy fosters the establishment of trust and enhances interpersonal connections.

- Maintaining Recollection of Names: Demonstrating attentiveness and respect during a conversation by consistently recalling and employing an individual's name.

Developing Meaningful Relationships through Casual Conversations:

Engaging in casual conversation can be a valuable foundation for cultivating significant connections when approached with genuine intent.

Discuss Personal Interests: When appropriate, engage in conversations about your interests and what ignites your enthusiasm. The quality of authenticity has the potential to serve as a source of inspiration for others, encouraging them also to express themselves openly.

Identify Common Interests: Discover shared interests that extend beyond superficial topics. This can facilitate deeper discussions and foster the exchange of shared experiences.

Provide Assistance and Support: When given a chance, extend help or support tailored to the individual's specific needs or difficulties. Promoting assistance cultivates a sense of mutual exchange.

Follow-up with a Personalized Touch: After the event, you should reach out to individuals with whom you established a connection by sending a personalized message. I want to express my appreciation for our recent conversation by highlighting a specific aspect that resonated with me.

Exploring the Psychological Dimensions of Persuasion through Casual Conversation:

Engaging in casual conversation can have a significant psychological influence on establishing connections.

The Principle of Liking: By demonstrating authentic interest and positive regard, one can activate the liking principle, which increases the likelihood of others reciprocating these sentiments.

The principle of reciprocity suggests that by sharing personal anecdotes or experiences, individuals are more inclined to reciprocate by opening up and sharing their own stories.

Mirroring and Rapport: Employing the technique of subtly mirroring the body language and tone of the other individual can effectively establish a sense of rapport and foster a comfortable environment.

The Halo Effect is a phenomenon whereby establishing a positive initial impression can result in individuals perceiving you more favorably during subsequent interactions.

In summary, developing proficiency in the art of small talk is a crucial competency for establishing significant connections at networking events. By actively participating in sincere and focused discussions, individuals can effectively generate a favorable influence, establish a memorable presence, and establish a foundation for more profound relationships. Engaging in small talk serves a purpose beyond casual conversation. It serves as a means to comprehend others, establish shared interests, and cultivate significant human connections that have the potential to result in valuable professional and personal associations. By recognizing the value of small talk, individuals can enhance their networking endeavors, leading to a more gratifying and advantageous outcome.

6.3 Following Up: From Exchange to Connection

The networking event has concluded, during which you actively participated in multiple conversations, forged valuable connections, and exchanged contact details. It is time to shift our focus from simply exchanging information to cultivating authentic relationships with the individuals we have encountered. This section will delve into practical strategies for post-networking event follow-up. We aim to convert those initial interactions into meaningful connections. Additionally, we will provide practical examples to illustrate each approach.

Customizing Your Follow-Up: When reaching out to someone for a follow-up, it is crucial to personalize your message to leave a lasting impression. It is advisable to refrain from using generic templates, as they may be perceived as lacking sincerity. Furthermore, it is advisable to incorporate a specific reference from your previous conversation to demonstrate your sincere engagement and interest in their thoughts and opinions. For example:

Dear [Name], It was a pleasure to have had the opportunity to meet you at the media conference yesterday. I greatly appreciated our discussion regarding the current industry trends and their significant impact on the advertising sector. I found your insights genuinely inspiring, and I would be interested in further discussing the topic over a coffee meeting shortly.

Enhancing Value: Strive to improve the value of your follow-up message by providing something pertinent to the recipient. You may consider providing an article or resource about a previously discussed topic, extending an invitation to an event that aligns with their interests, or even offering a referral or introduction to someone in your network who could be of value to them.

Hello [Name], I trust that you are in good health. I recall our previous conversation about innovative marketing strategies. I have encountered an article that I believe would be highly relevant to your interests. Please find the provided link below: Please see the article link attached. You will likely find it to be informative and thought-provoking. Please inform me if you would like to discuss this matter further.

Establishing Connections on Social Media: Actively engaging with new contacts on various social media platforms, particularly LinkedIn, presents an excellent opportunity to foster and sustain professional relationships while remaining informed about each other's career advancements. When establishing a connection, it is advisable to include a personalized message as a gentle reminder of the upcoming meeting.

Hello [Name], I thoroughly enjoyed our encounter at last week's entertainment industry event. I was particularly impressed by your extensive background in production and your innovative approach. I would greatly appreciate maintaining a connection with you and exploring potential avenues for mutual support in the future.

Requesting a Follow-Up Meeting: If you have engaged in a significant conversation with an individual, it is advisable to propose a follow-up meeting to explore potential collaboration further or engage in a more in-depth discussion regarding shared interests.

Hello [Name], Our discussion regarding the difficulties encountered by media professionals in the digital era was enlightening. I would appreciate the opportunity to further our conversation during a more informal lunch meeting. Could you kindly confirm your availability for next week on either Tuesday or Thursday?

Cultivating the Relationship: Establishing and maintaining meaningful connections requires continuous effort. Maintain and develop your relationships by regularly initiating contact with your contacts, sharing pertinent updates, and extending congratulations for their accomplishments. It is important to emphasize that the maintenance of a network necessitates a sincere commitment and genuine interest in the success of others.

Dear [Name], I trust that everything is proceeding smoothly. I noted your recent promotion and would like to express my sincere congratulations. Your commitment and diligent efforts are deserving of commendation. I propose that we schedule a meeting shortly to commemorate your achievements.

The Importance of Face-to-Face Meetings: Although digital communication offers convenience, there is no substitute for in-person interactions. Whenever feasible, take advantage of opportunities to personally engage with your professional network by arranging face-to-face meetings over coffee, lunch, or industry-related gatherings. Face-to-face meetings enhance interpersonal relationships and cultivate a more profound connection.

Dear [Name], I hope you are well. I found our discussion at the advertising summit to be quite enjoyable, and I believe there may be potential for us to explore mutually beneficial collaboration opportunities. I propose arranging a meeting over coffee next week to delve deeper into this matter. Which day would be most convenient for you?

Following up after networking events is a crucial link that elevates casual interactions into valuable connections. By incorporating personalization into your messages, providing valuable content, and cultivating your established relationships, you will foster a network that flourishes through authentic care and mutual assistance. It is essential to recognize that networking extends beyond mere transactions. It entails establishing a community comprising individuals with similar professional interests and goals, fostering an environment of mutual support and inspiration. To enhance your networking experience, it is advisable to adopt a proactive, authentic, and attentive approach in your follow-up interactions. By doing so, you will discover that networking can be a fulfilling and gratifying endeavor.

"The struggle you're in today is developing the strength you need for tomorrow." - Robert Tew

Summary

You just completed chapter 6 of this book, networking expert! The networking etiquette and best practices detailed in this chapter have prepared you to make connections easily. Congratulations on learning to approach strangers confidently, make pleasant small talk, and follow up with people you might want to connect with.

You should know that networking is about building genuine relationships, not just doing business with people. We've busted some popular myths about networking and embraced the human-to-human part.

Remember that the keys to success are genuine interest, active listening, and making an excellent first impression. You have the tools to make a lasting impression at industry meetings, coffee breaks, or even within your own company.

So, use these pointers to go into the world confidently and watch your network grow. Your future will be shaped by the people you meet today. If you keep networking with heart, there will be no limits to what you can do. On to great things in networking!

Multiple Choice Questions

1, What is one practical way to cultivate self-confidence when approaching strangers at networking events?

a) Substitute self-doubt with positive affirmations and recall strengths.

b) Avoid setting clear goals and expectations for the event.

c) Pretend to be someone else to appear more appealing.

d) Disregard individual qualities and focus solely on self-interest.

2. Why is active listening important during small talk conversations?

a) It allows you to check your mobile device for potential distractions.

b) It demonstrates a lack of interest in the speaker's opinions.

c) It shows genuine engagement and respect for the speaker's viewpoint.

d) It helps you scan the surroundings for potential connections.

3. What is the primary purpose of engaging in small talk during networking events?

a) To establish genuine human connections that go beyond superficial exchanges.

b) To showcase one's knowledge and expertise on various topics.

c) To impress others with elaborate stories and anecdotes.

d) To demonstrate assertiveness and confidence to make an immediate impact.

4. What is one way to make a memorable impression during small talk interactions?

a) Employ humor excessively to entertain others.

b) Demonstrate empathy and compassion towards others.

c) Avoid using the individual's name in the conversation.

d) Share personal experiences to dominate the conversation.

5. What does the Halo Effect refer to in the context of small talk and networking?

a) The phenomenon of people forgetting names after a networking event.

b) The tendency of people to recall shared interests during small talk.

c) The influence of positive initial impressions on subsequent interactions.

d) The practice of mirroring body language to establish rapport.

6. When following up after networking events, what is essential to make a lasting impression?

a) Using generic templates for messages to maintain professionalism.

b) Incorporating specific references from previous conversations.

c) Providing vague and non-personalized content to avoid intruding.

d) Sending messages without mentioning the event where you met.

7. How can you enhance the value of your follow-up message after networking?

a) Provide something irrelevant and unrelated to the recipient.

b) Avoid any further contact to avoid appearing too eager.

c) Offer something pertinent to the recipient, like an article or event invitation.

d) Request assistance or favors to build a mutual exchange.

8. What is the primary goal of engaging in face-to-face meetings with networking contacts?

a) To avoid engaging in digital communication that lacks convenience.

b) To create a comfortable environment for casual conversations.

c) To establish a genuine human connection and foster deeper relationships.

d) To minimize the impact of first impressions and focus on long-term interactions.

9. What is the importance of practicing active listening during small talk?

a) It allows you to plan your responses while the speaker talks.

b) It shows that you are disinterested in the conversation.

c) It helps establish rapport and engage genuinely with the speaker.

d) It demonstrates a lack of empathy and understanding.

10. Why is it essential to personalize follow-up messages after networking events?

a) To showcase your creativity in writing messages.

b) To appear more formal and professional in your communication.

c) To demonstrate sincere engagement and interest in the recipient.

d) To avoid spending too much time on networking activities.

Answers

1. a

2. c

3. a

4. b

5. c,d

6. b

7. c

8. c

9. c

10. c

Chapter 7: Networking Within Your Organization

Welcome to the seventh chapter of "Network Like a Pro: The Ultimate Guide to Successful Networking at Industry Events." This chapter will examine the effectiveness of networking within your organization. Building relationships within your organization is equally essential as networking externally, as it can lead to various development, collaboration, and career advancement opportunities. I will share strategies for making the most of internal networking and establishing meaningful connections with leaders, colleagues, and mentors based on my experiences and observations.

"The currency of real networking is not greed but generosity." - Keith Ferrazzi

7.1 The Power of Internal Networking

Benefits of Internal Networking:

Internal networking involves developing relationships with coworkers, supervisors, and mentors. This strategy enables you to utilize your organization's diverse expertise, knowledge, and resources. Connecting with individuals from different departments gives you a more comprehensive understanding of your organization's operations and potential collaboration opportunities.

Breaking down Silos:

Internal networking's ability to break down departmental divisions to improve collaboration is one of its primary advantages. When employees collaborate and share insights across different divisions, it fosters a culture of cooperation, resulting in enhanced problem-solving, innovation, and decision-making efficiency.

Building rapport:

Internal networking isn't just about exchanging business cards or making superficial connections; it's about establishing trust and rapport with coworkers. Sincere relationships facilitate open communication, which makes it simpler to exchange ideas, seek advice, and promote one another's professional development.

While formal meetings and company events are essential for networking, informal interactions are just as beneficial. Participate in casual conversations during coffee breaks, team-building exercises, and virtual social gatherings. These everyday conditions are frequently more conducive to forming personal relationships.

Utilizing Mentorship for Personal Growth:

Internal networking can lead to mentorship opportunities. Seeking advice from seasoned coworkers or senior executives can expedite your professional development and provide valuable insights on advancing your career.

Company Culture:

By actively participating in internal networking, you enhance the company's culture. Positive employee relationships foster a supportive environment, which increases job satisfaction and decreases employee turnover.

Practicing Proactivity:

Engaging in internal networking demonstrates your initiative and initiative within your organization. It shows your commitment to personal development, willingness to collaborate, and dedication to the organization's success.

Embracing Diversity and Inclusion

Internal networking allows you to connect with individuals from various cultures, origins, and experiences. Acceptance of this diversity promotes inclusiveness and creates a more dynamic and inventive workplace.

Employees who network actively within the organization contribute to developing a learning organization. Sharing information becomes ingrained in the company's culture, resulting in continuous product and industry-specific adaptation.

Utilizing Internal Networks for Career Progression: Internal networking can significantly impact your career progression. By cultivating relationships with key decision-makers and influential individuals within your organization, you increase your visibility and position yourself to take advantage of potential opportunities.

Internal networking is a potent instrument that should not be overlooked. You can unlock many possibilities for professional growth, collaboration, and career advancement by proactively interacting with your organization's colleagues, leaders, and mentors. Accept the human-to-human approach in your internal networking efforts, and you will find that the relationships you establish within your company will open doors to new opportunities, personal development, and a more rewarding and fulfilling career path. Remember that your network within the company is an invaluable resource that can contribute to your professional success and help your company grow.

7.2 Creating Opportunities through Cross-Departmental Collaboration

Explore the power of interdepartmental collaboration and how it can unleash opportunities for your organization. Collaboration across teams and departments is more than a buzzword; it is a strategic approach that can drive innovation, increase productivity, and cultivate a more inclusive and dynamic workplace. We will examine diverse methods for developing cross-departmental relationships and leveraging them to create meaningful personal and professional development opportunities using real-world examples and expert insights.

Breaking Down Barriers: Accepting Diverse Points of View

Effective interdepartmental collaboration begins with eliminating the barriers that frequently exist between teams. Engage with coworkers from different departments, seeking their perspectives and learning about their challenges and successes. You open the door to novel concepts and creative solutions by embracing various perspectives.

During a company-wide ideation session, you contact members of various departments, such as marketing, design, and finance. By valuing their input, you can unearth original insights that result in a ground-breaking campaign strategy.

Seeking Common Objectives: Aligning Goals for Success

Consider opportunities in which the objectives of multiple departments align. Identifying shared objectives facilitates collaboration and ensures that efforts are complementary rather than redundant. Working toward common goals together fosters a sense of camaraderie and mutual support. For example, in preparation for a prominent industry event, you help sales and marketing teams to develop a unified messaging strategy. By coordinating your efforts, you can maximize their impact and establish a consistent brand presence.

Participation in Cross-Functional Projects: Expanding Skill Sets

Participate in cross-functional initiatives in which employees from various departments collaborate as a unified unit. These initiatives allow you to expand your skill sets, gain exposure to the knowledge of others, and demonstrate your abilities outside of your immediate team.

You volunteer to participate in an interdepartmental task force focusing on process optimization. Through this collaboration, you gain valuable insights into workflow management and a reputation as a versatile team member.

Lunch and Learn Sessions: Building Bridges Through Informal Interactions

Informal interactions, such as "lunch and learn" sessions, should be used to foster interdepartmental relationships. These informal gatherings allow employees to share their knowledge, experiences, and recent accomplishments, fostering a culture of continuous learning and mutual support.

Example: You orchestrate a "lunch and learn" session in which members from various departments discuss the latest industry trends. This initiative strengthens professional relationships and generates creative ideas for future endeavors.

Celebrating and Recognizing Success: Promoting Collaboration

Recognize and celebrate effective interdepartmental collaborations to inspire additional teamwork and cooperation. Not only does recognition enhance morale, but it also reinforces the worth of collective efforts.

After a successful product launch that required contributions from multiple departments, you recognize and appreciate the collaborative efforts of all involved parties. This acknowledgment generates a positive feedback loop that encourages future interdepartmental collaborations.

Mentoring Across Departments: Knowledge Sharing

Opportunities for mentoring should not be restricted to a single department. Offer mentorship or seek out mentorship from teammates on opposing teams. Sharing knowledge and experiences can lead to insightful realizations and personal development.

You connect with a senior colleague from a different department with extensive project management experience. You acquire valuable insights into efficient project execution and organizational dynamics through this mentoring.

Collaboration across departments is a potent catalyst for personal and professional development within your organization. You support collaboration and innovation by actively seeking diverse perspectives, aligning objectives, engaging in cross-functional initiatives, and building bridges through informal interactions. Embrace the opportunities to learn from and support colleagues across departments. You will discover a world of possibilities and career advancement that the power of collaboration is waiting to unleash. Individuals benefit from inclusive and synergistic collaboration, contributing to your organization's overall success and resiliency. Therefore, seize the opportunity to network and collaborate with coworkers from different departments and observe as your network grows and your career soars to new heights.

7.3 Building Relationships with Leaders and Mentors

Explore the art of developing relationships with organizational leaders and mentors. Cultivating these meaningful relationships can be a game-changer for your career development, as it opens doors to invaluable advice, assistance, and opportunities. This section will discuss strategies for becoming more likable and influential, cultivating strong relationships with mentors and guides, and maintaining these relationships for long-term success.

Being pleasant and Influential: Being affable is essential to establishing solid relationships within your organization. Here are some suggestions for enhancing your popularity and influence:

Take the time to actively listen to others and demonstrate genuine interest in their thoughts and ideas. Make them feel heard and valued.

Practice Empathy and Comprehension: Consider the difficulties and experiences of your colleagues with empathy. Empathy cultivates trust and nurtures a supportive environment.

Exude Confidence Without Arrogance: Exude confidence in your skills and ideas while avoiding arrogance and condescension. Confidence is attractive, whereas arrogance repels others.

Master the Art of Small Talk Meaningful small talk can aid in establishing rapport and fostering a welcoming environment. Discover shared interests and use them to connect on a personal level.

Be a Team Player: Demonstrate collaboration and support for others. Being a team member will earn you the respect and admiration of your peers.

Attracting Support and Assistance:

To encourage people to assist and assist you, emphasize reciprocity and mutual benefit:

Provide Assistance: Be proactive in offering your colleagues assistance and support whenever feasible. By demonstrating your willingness to help, you create an environment where others are likelier to return the favor.

Be Dependable and Reliable: Establish a reputation for dependability by honoring commitments and keeping promises. People are more likely to assist those in whom they have faith.

Don't neglect to express appreciation when others assist. A straightforward "thank you" can do much to strengthen relationships.

Developing Relationships with Mentors and Advisors:

Finding mentors and advisers within your organization can substantially affect your professional development. How to establish and maintain these relationships:

Identify Potential Mentors: Identify individuals whose knowledge aligns with your objectives and values. This could include senior leaders, seasoned colleagues, or even peers with valuable insights to share.

Seek Authentic Connections: Be genuine and sincere when approaching potential mentors. Share your goals and demonstrate your enthusiasm to gain knowledge from their experiences.

Accept Constructive Feedback: Welcome feedback from your mentors and advisers. It is an opportunity for personal development and advancement.

Keep in Touch: Maintain consistent contact with your mentors. Schedule periodic check-ins or casual catch-ups to maintain communication and knowledge.

Developing Long-Term Connections:

Developing strong connections with leaders and mentors is a continuous process. How to maintain these relationships:

Continue attending company events, seminars, and networking opportunities to maintain relationships with mentors and guides.

Provide Updates: Inform your mentors of your progress and accomplishments. Sharing your achievements and obstacles facilitates their comprehension of your development voyage.

Demonstrate gratitude for the assistance and support you have received. A handwritten note or heartfelt email can strengthen your relationship with your mentors.

Consider becoming a mentor to others after you have benefited from mentorship. Not only does paying it forward help others, but it also enhances your understanding of the topic.

Relationship building with leaders and mentors is essential to your career development voyage. You make a supportive and collaborative work environment by being courteous, influential, and helpful to others. For long-term success, seek mentors who can guide and support, and cultivate these relationships. Remember that networking isn't just about what others can do for you; it's about establishing authentic, mutually beneficial relationships. Adopt a human-to-human approach, and you'll find that your network grows with meaningful connections that enhance your professional life. Therefore, take the initiative to cultivate relationships with leaders and mentors and observe as these connections are the foundation of your successful career.

"You can have everything in life you want if you will just help enough other people get what they want." - Zig Ziglar

Summary

The power of networking within your company has been unlocked in Chapter 7, and you now have the information you need to create opportunities, build solid cross-department partnerships, and build relationships with leaders and mentors.

Good for you now that you have realized how crucial internal networking is. The real magic happens inside your business. You can grow and advance in your job by getting to know your coworkers and mentors.

Keep building these relationships and look for ways to work with people from other areas. Don't forget that networking within your company helps your career and gives you a sense of belonging and support.

So, go out and make connections at work like a pro. The people you meet today will have a significant impact on your future. Internal networking is a powerful tool to help your business reach new heights.

Multiple Choice Questions

1. What is one of the primary advantages of internal networking within an organization?

a) Gaining access to external industry events.

b) Increasing competition among departments.

c) Breaking down departmental divisions for better collaboration.

d) Focusing solely on personal development.

2. How does internal networking contribute to a positive company culture?

a) By fostering a sense of competition and individual achievement.

b) By encouraging employees to work independently and avoid collaboration.

c) By promoting positive employee relationships and mutual support.

d) By creating silos and limiting communication between departments.

3. What is one way to make the most of informal interactions for internal networking?

a) Avoid participating in coffee breaks or social gatherings.

b) Only engage in formal meetings and company events for

networking.

c) Be actively present and participate in conversations during informal gatherings.

d) Focus solely on exchanging business cards and contact details.

4. How can internal networking lead to mentorship opportunities?

a) By avoiding any interaction with senior executives or seasoned coworkers.

b) By seeking advice and insights from colleagues in different departments.

c) By limiting interactions to your immediate team members.

d) By disregarding the importance of personal growth and development.

5. What is one strategy for effective interdepartmental collaboration?

a) Emphasizing departmental divisions to maintain focus on individual goals.

b) Seeking diverse perspectives and embracing various points of view.

c) Encouraging redundancy in efforts to achieve common objectives.

d) Avoiding cross-functional projects to stay within your immediate team's scope.

6. Why is it essential to identify shared objectives when collaborating across departments?

a) To ensure redundancy and unnecessary competition between departments.

b) To foster a sense of isolation and lack of cooperation.

c) To align efforts and facilitate collaboration towards common goals.

d) To minimize communication and maintain departmental divisions.

7. How can informal interactions, like "lunch and learn" sessions, contribute to interdepartmental relationships?

a) By providing an opportunity to avoid interaction with coworkers from other departments.

b) By encouraging employees to work individually and avoid sharing knowledge.

c) By fostering a culture of continuous learning and mutual support.

d) By limiting communication to formal settings only.

8. How can recognizing and celebrating interdepartmental collaborations benefit an organization?

a) It fosters a culture of competition and individual recognition.

b) It reduces employee morale and discourages further collaboration.

c) It reinforces the value of collective efforts and inspires future teamwork.

d) It encourages isolation and lack of support between departments.

9. How can individuals benefit from inclusive and synergistic collaboration across departments?

a) By avoiding cross-functional projects to maintain a narrow skill set.

b) By focusing solely on personal objectives and ignoring team goals.

c) By expanding skill sets, gaining exposure to diverse knowledge, and showcasing abilities.

d) By neglecting to seek guidance from coworkers in different departments.

10. What is the significance of embracing diversity and inclusion in internal networking?

a) It encourages silos and limited communication within the organization.

b) It creates a dynamic and inventive workplace that values different perspectives.

c) It fosters competition and rivalry among employees.

d) It promotes isolation and lack of cooperation between departments.

Answers

1. c

2. c

3. c

4. b

5. b

6. c

7. c

8. c

9. c

10. d

Chapter 8: Networking Beyond Your Company

Chapter 8 of the book "Network Like a Pro: The Ultimate Guide to Successful Networking at Industry Events" delves into networking beyond the confines of one's organization, presenting a comprehensive exploration of the extensive opportunities available in this domain. Individuals can expand their network of contacts and potential collaborators by actively participating in professional organizations, industry groups, conferences, seminars, and volunteering activities. Let us explore each avenue and ascertain how you can optimize these opportunities to enhance your career and influence your industry favorably.

"Opportunities don't happen. You create them." - Chris Grosser

8.1 Joining Professional Associations and Industry Groups

Explore the realm of professional associations and industry groups. These organizations provide exceptional opportunities for networking, sharing knowledge, and advancing one's career. This section will examine a systematic approach to becoming a member of these associations, establishing a noteworthy presence, and cultivating enduring relationships.

Step 1: Conduct thorough research to identify associations relevant to your field or industry.

Research professional associations and industry groups aligning with your expertise, career objectives, and interests. Please search for reputable organizations in your industry known for promoting collaboration and maintaining high standards of excellence. It is advisable to consider national and local chapters to optimize networking opportunities.

Step 2: Participate in association events and networking sessions.

Once you have identified the relevant associations, it is advisable to attend their events and networking sessions regularly. These events offer chances to network with professionals with similar interests and influential figures in the industry. It is advisable to take the initiative in introducing oneself, exchanging business cards, and demonstrating a sincere interest in the work of others.

Step 3: Participate enthusiastically in discussions and workshops.

It is highly recommended to actively engage in discussions, workshops, and panel sessions during association events. Please contribute your expertise and insights to establish yourself as a knowledgeable and valuable community member. Maintaining an open mindset and actively seeking opportunities to learn from others is essential. Doing so can effectively broaden your knowledge base and enhance your understanding in various areas.

Step 4: Pursue Leadership Positions:

As you progress in your involvement with the association, it is advisable to contemplate pursuing leadership positions. Participating in committees or boards not only increases your visibility but also enables you to make valuable contributions to the organization's growth and strategic direction. Leadership positions provide valuable networking opportunities with influential individuals.

Step 5: Share Your Professional Knowledge:

Please extend an offer to deliver presentations at association events or contribute articles to their publications. By sharing your expertise, you can establish yourself as a respected authority in your industry, garnering attention from peers, potential employers, and potential collaborators. Contributing to association publications can also facilitate the establishment of valuable connections with fellow contributors.

Step 6: Leverage Online Networking Platforms:

Utilize social media and online networking platforms to establish connections with association members in the interim periods between events. Participate in industry-related discussions, disseminate valuable content, and actively engage with others' posts to maintain a prominent presence within the community.

Step 7: Conduct a follow-up and maintain regular communication:

Engaging in post-networking event communication is advisable by sending personalized messages or emails to establish and nurture connections with new contacts. Thank you for your valuable time and insightful contributions. We greatly appreciate your input. Moving forward, we would like to explore potential avenues for collaboration or further discussion.

Step 8: Participate in yearly meetings and special events.

Prioritizing attendance at the association's annual conferences and special events is highly recommended. These larger gatherings provide a more comprehensive range of networking opportunities and the potential to connect with influential figures within the industry.

Step 9: Provide Assistance and Guidance:

As you establish your presence within the association, it is recommended that you extend your support and mentorship to newer members or individuals who are seeking guidance. By demonstrating a willingness to allocate your time and share your expertise generously, you enhance your standing as a highly regarded individual within the community.

Step 10: Participate in Collaborative Projects:

Please actively seek out opportunities to participate in collaborative projects with fellow association members. Collaborative efforts have the potential to yield innovative solutions, increased visibility, and more robust industry connections.

Participating in professional associations and industry groups provides individuals with valuable opportunities to establish connections with various contacts, mentors, and potential collaborators. By actively participating in multiple events, actively pursuing leadership positions, making valuable contributions based on your expertise, and utilizing online networking platforms, you can establish enduring connections that facilitate career advancement and enhance professional growth. It is important to note that joining these associations encompasses more than personal gains. It entails positively contributing to the industry and fostering a robust network that benefits all stakeholders. Adopting a systematic approach that involves joining, engaging, and growing within professional associations is advisable to expand and advance your career. By following this step-by-step method, you will witness the expansion of your network and the subsequent elevation of your job to unprecedented levels.

8.2 Attending Conferences and Seminars

In this section, we will delve into the effective utilization of conferences and seminars, the advantages of attending these events, and techniques for establishing enduring professional relationships.

Preparing for the Event:

Before attending a conference or seminar, it is advisable to adequately allocate sufficient time to prepare for the upcoming experience.

Please research the agenda. Please take the time to familiarize yourself with the event agenda and carefully identify sessions and workshops that align with your specific interests and professional goals.

Establish Objectives:

Establish clear objectives for attending the event. Clearly defined goals will enable you to optimize your time, whether for gaining valuable insights into industry trends, expanding your professional network by connecting with potential collaborators or exploring new opportunities.

Carry Business Cards/Portfolio:

Please bring an adequate supply of business cards to facilitate networking and exchanging contact information with other participants. These compact paper items can potentially serve as your means of establishing enduring connections.

Actively Engage:

Demonstrate active engagement during conference sessions and workshops by proactively interacting with the speakers and fellow participants.

Ask Questions:

Engage in Q&A sessions by posing thoughtful questions to acquire profound insights and showcase your active involvement.

Utilize Break Times for Networking:

Take advantage of coffee breaks, lunchtime, and networking receptions as opportunities to engage in conversations with fellow attendees. When engaging with individuals, adopting a friendly and approachable attitude is advisable while demonstrating a sincere interest in their professional endeavors.

Try to learn:

Take the opportunity to learn from industry experts and peers by being open to new ideas. It is advisable to maintain an open mindset towards new perspectives, as they have the potential to stimulate innovative ideas within your professional endeavors.

Utilizing Social Media:

Social media has the potential to enhance your conference experience significantly:

Utilize Event Hashtags:

Monitor event hashtags on platforms like Twitter and LinkedIn to remain informed about ongoing discussions and engage with fellow participants in the virtual space.

Please consider sharing your valuable insights and key takeaways from the event on your social media platforms. Participating in online discussions can expand your networking opportunities beyond the confines of a conference venue.

Strategies for Optimizing Networking Opportunities:

Networking plays a pivotal role in participating in conferences and seminars. Here is a guide on how to maximize these opportunities:

Demonstrate Approachability: Display a warm smile and maintain an open and inviting body language, fostering an environment encouraging others to approach you easily.

When initiating a self-introduction, kindly provide your name, professional experience, and express your enthusiasm towards the event's subject matter.

Demonstrate Effective Listening Skills: Engage in active listening when individuals share their experiences and insights. Demonstrate authentic curiosity in the content they are sharing.

Contact Information Exchange: Following engaging and meaningful conversations, exchanging contact information with individuals you wish to maintain a connection with is advisable.

Advantages of Participating in Conferences and Seminars:

- Participating in conferences and seminars provides numerous benefits:
- Networking Opportunities: Conferences serve as a platform for professionals from various backgrounds to convene, offering valuable networking opportunities.
- Knowledge Expansion: Acquire valuable insights into recent trends, industry best practices, and innovative advancements.
- Career Advancement: Establish meaningful relationships with prospective mentors, collaborators, or employers who possess the potential to enhance your professional trajectory significantly.

- Seeking inspiration and motivation can be achieved by engaging with industry thought leaders and peers. This interaction can reignite one's passion for their chosen profession.
- Professional Development: Gaining knowledge from peers and being open to innovative concepts nurtures personal and career advancement.

Participating in conferences and seminars is a worthwhile investment in professional growth. These events offer a multitude of benefits beyond knowledge acquisition. They provide valuable opportunities for networking with individuals who share similar interests, fostering inspiration, and discovering new avenues for growth and exploration. To optimize your conference experience, it is advisable to make thorough preparations in advance, actively participate in sessions, utilize social media platforms effectively, and capitalize on networking opportunities. Adopting a human-to-human approach in your interactions can catalyze personal and career growth. I encourage you to venture beyond your comfort zone and fully engage in the conference environment. By doing so, you will witness the formation of valuable connections that can open up numerous opportunities and foster a robust network to support your path to achievement.

8.3 Volunteering and Giving Back

Volunteering provides distinct networking opportunities and the chance to develop meaningful relationships with like-minded individuals. In this section, we will discuss the advantages of volunteering, strategies for impactful engagement, and the long-lasting relationships that can be forged through charitable giving.

Finding Causes That Align with Your Values:

Start your journey as a volunteer by identifying causes that align with your values and interests. Whether environmental conservation, education, social welfare, or any other reason near and dear to your heart, choosing a cause that correlates with your interests guarantees a fulfilling and meaningful experience.

Engaging with Nonprofit Organizations Once you have identified a cause, you should seek out reputable nonprofit organizations operating in that field. Engage with them to learn about their initiatives, ongoing projects, and how you can contribute your time, talents, or resources.

Many nonprofit organizations organize volunteer events, community initiatives, and fundraising activities. Participate in these events to become actively involved in the cause and to network with other volunteers who share your enthusiasm.

Networking with Other Volunteers: Participate in meaningful conversations with other volunteers at volunteer events. Share your reasons for participating and listen to their perspectives and experiences. These interactions may result in long-lasting alliances and professional ties.

Providing Your Skills and Knowledge: Leverage your professional abilities and expertise to have a significant impact. Your expertise can be a helpful resource for nonprofit organizations, whether through pro bono consulting, offering seminars, or contributing creative talents.

Consider Pursuing Leadership Roles in Nonprofits: As you develop trust and rapport within a nonprofit organization, you should assume leadership roles. You may add to the organization's vision, work alongside influential individuals, and expand your network by serving on committees or boards.

Participating in Fundraising and Networking Events: Many nonprofits host fundraising and networking events. Participate in these events to network with influential individuals, prospective partners, and advocates who share a commitment to the exact cause.

Connecting with Nonprofit Leaders and Organizers: Communicate with nonprofit leaders and organizers. Express your desire to support their cause and investigate possible collaborations. Developing relationships with these leaders can lead to new opportunities in the nonprofit sector.

Building a Reputation as a Helpful Volunteer: Demonstrate your dedication to the cause by being dependable, devoted, and proactive in your volunteer work. Your credibility will increase within the organization and among your peers if you have a positive reputation as a helpful and involved volunteer.

Consider becoming a mentor to new volunteers or encouraging coworkers and acquaintances to join you in giving back once you have experienced the benefits of volunteering. In addition to strengthening your connections, paying it forward generates a positive cascading effect within your network.

Offering and giving back to the community is a transformative endeavor that benefits the causes you support and provides unique networking opportunities. By engaging with nonprofit organizations, participating in volunteer events, and networking with other volunteers and leaders, you can forge meaningful relationships based on shared values and a desire to make a difference. Adopt a human-to-human approach in your interactions, demonstrate a sincere interest in the cause, and share your skills and expertise to make a lasting impact. As you devote your time and energy to meaningful causes, you'll find that the connections you make through volunteering form the basis of a flourishing, purpose-driven network. Therefore, embark on your journey of giving back, and observe as these connections enrich your personal and professional life, cultivating a sense of fulfillment and satisfaction in positively impacting the world around you.

Key Takeaways from Chapter 8: Networking Outside of Your Company

Join a professional group or association.

- Find industry-related groups and companies to add to your network.
- Attend events and get involved to meet other people in your field. Go to meetings and seminars.
- Research the speakers and attendees ahead of time to get ready.
- Set goals for networking, make absolute links and then keep in touch. Help out and give back:
- Find ways to help that fit with your interests and skills.
- Help causes you to care about while making new friends.

Use social networks:

- Use your LinkedIn page to show off what you know.
- Join meaningful online discussions and talk to people in your network.

How to Make Lasting Friends:

- Focus on making genuine relationships instead of collecting names and numbers.
- When caring for relationships, give help and stay the same.

Balance Efforts to network:

- Use your time well and focus on having good conversations.
- Find a good balance between networking tasks you can do online and offline.

Accept differences:

- Talk to people from different fields and backgrounds.
- Accept other points of view to find new ideas and chances.

Become more open-minded:

- Meet people outside of your comfort zone and look into new fields.
- Attend events that bring together people from different areas to learn more.

Keep making connections while keeping an open mind and a friendly attitude. Your contacts will lead you to exciting opportunities and complete your career more enjoyable. Stay interested and honest; your network will grow, giving you access to unique possibilities.

Multiple Choice Questions

1. What is the first step in joining a professional association or industry group?

a) Attend their events and networking sessions.

b) Seek out reputable nonprofit organizations.

c) Conduct thorough research to identify relevant associations.

d) Provide assistance and guidance to newer members.

2. How can attending conferences and seminars benefit your career?

a) By avoiding social interactions and focusing solely on learning.

b) By establishing objectives and preparing thoroughly for the event.

c) By limiting participation to Q&A sessions with speakers.

d) By solely utilizing social media platforms to engage with the event.

3. How can you optimize networking opportunities at conferences and seminars?

a) By avoiding engaging in conversations with other participants.

b) By demonstrating approachability and effective listening skills.

c) By solely focusing on gaining knowledge from industry experts.

d) By refraining from exchanging contact information with new connections.

4. What is one strategy for establishing enduring connections while volunteering?

a) Avoid engaging in meaningful conversations with other volunteers.

b) Offer financial support to nonprofit organizations without actively participating.

c) Utilize social media hashtags to connect with nonprofit leaders.

d) Engage in meaningful conversations and share reasons for volunteering.

5. How can volunteering and giving back positively impact your professional network?

a) By limiting connections to fellow volunteers at events.

b) By establishing relationships with nonprofit leaders and organizers.

c) By focusing solely on fundraising events for networking opportunities.

d) By disregarding the importance of demonstrating professional skills.

6. How can joining committees or boards within a nonprofit organization benefit your networking efforts?

a) By limiting your visibility and interactions with other volunteers.

b) By reducing your chances of assuming leadership roles within the organization.

c) By providing networking opportunities with influential individuals.

d) By avoiding participation in community initiatives and volunteer events.

7. What is one advantage of using social media during conferences and seminars?

a) It helps you avoid face-to-face interactions with other attendees.

b) It allows you to monitor event hashtags for ongoing discussions.

c) It limits your exposure to industry insights and trends.

d) It avoids sharing insights and key takeaways from the event.

8. How can you demonstrate effective networking at industry events?

a) By maintaining a closed mindset and refusing to accept new perspectives.

b) By solely exchanging business cards without engaging in conversations.

c) By demonstrating approachability, active listening, and exchanging contact information.

d) By avoiding engaging with speakers and fellow participants during sessions.

9. Why is it essential to adopt a human-to-human approach in networking efforts?

a) To focus solely on individual gains and ignore the needs of others.

b) To limit interactions with people from different fields and backgrounds.

c) To foster genuine relationships and cultivate a supportive network.

d) To disregard the significance of attending events and seminars.

10. What is the significance of finding causes that align with your values when volunteering?

a) It limits your involvement and commitment to nonprofit organizations.

b) It ensures a fulfilling and meaningful experience as a volunteer.

c) It discourages engaging in networking and forming connections with other volunteers.

d) It prevents you from offering your skills and expertise to the cause.

Answers

1. c

2. b

3. b

4. d

5. b

6. c

7. b

8. c

8. c

10. b

Chapter 9: Overcoming Networking Challenges

The following chapter will discuss prevalent networking obstacles and offer valuable insights on effective strategies to overcome them. Networking can be daunting for individuals new to it or encountering specific challenges. However, by adopting the appropriate mindset and employing effective strategies, one can successfully navigate any networking situation with poise and self-assurance.

"To know someone here or there with whom you can feel there is understanding in spite of distances or thoughts expressed - that can make this life a garden." - Johann Wolfgang von Goethe

9.1 Introversion and Networking

Embracing Your Authentic Self: Authenticity is a valuable attribute when it comes to networking. Embrace your authentic self and allow your genuine personality to radiate.

Recognize and Embrace Your Strengths:

Take a moment to contemplate your distinctive strengths and skills, and take pride in the valuable contributions you offer. It is essential to acknowledge that one's individuality is a distinguishing factor.

Maintain Authenticity in Your Interactions:

Refrain from presenting a false persona or attempting to portray yourself as someone you are not. Sincerity and authenticity are highly valued attributes in the realm of networking.

Please feel free to discuss your personal passions and interests outside of work. Engaging in the sharing of personal interests can foster more profound connections with individuals.

Enhancing Self-Assurance in Networking Scenarios:

Having confidence is of utmost importance when it comes to networking. Utilize psychological strategies to enhance self-assurance and establish a memorable impact:

Power Poses: Power poses are recommended to enhance one's confidence before participating in networking events. Assume a confident posture by standing upright with your chest lifted and briefly placing your hands on your hips. This action can help stimulate a feeling of empowerment.

Visualization: Engage in the practice of visualizing fruitful networking interactions. Envision yourself actively participating in conversations with confidence and establishing meaningful connections.

Utilize positive affirmations as a preparatory practice before engaging in networking events. Encourage yourself to acknowledge your capabilities, likability, and inherent value.

Establish Realistic Goals: Establish attainable networking objectives for each event. It is essential to acknowledge and commemorate your achievements, regardless of their perceived magnitude.

Managing Imposter Syndrome:

Imposter syndrome is a prevalent phenomenon; however, it should not impede your ability to engage in networking activities. Address the challenge at hand by implementing the following strategies:

Acknowledge Your Accomplishments: Take a moment to reflect on the milestones you have achieved and your diligent efforts to attain your present professional standing.

Seeking Supportive Feedback: Conversed with mentors or trusted individuals who can offer constructive feedback and validate your skills and capabilities.

Emphasize Learning Opportunities: Regard networking as a valuable occasion to gain knowledge from others rather than solely as an opportunity to showcase your abilities.

Utilizing Cognitive Techniques to Positively Influence Individuals:

In networking, possessing the knowledge and skills to influence others positively and effectively can significantly contribute to establishing successful connections.

Use mirroring techniques to subtly align your body language, tone, and pace with the person you are conversing with. This can foster a sense of familiarity and establish rapport.

Active Listening: Engage in active listening to demonstrate a sincere interest in the perspectives and thoughts of others. Ask their thoughts and experiences by posing open-ended questions for more extensive sharing.

Provide genuine compliments and validation to individuals. Expressing appreciation can foster a sense of value and increase the likelihood of active participation from individuals.

Enhancing Confidence through Mind Tricks: Utilizing specific techniques to manipulate your mindset can improve confidence levels during networking interactions.

Utilizing Power Poses: As previously discussed, the act of adopting power poses has the potential to elicit sensations of self-assurance and authority.

Visualization: Envision yourself embodying a poised and accomplished networker who is liked by everyone and a person people want to talk to. The act of visualizing enhances the likelihood of materializing one's desired outcome.

The significance of dressing appropriately cannot be overstated, as it has the potential to significantly enhance one's confidence and leave a favorable initial impression.

Networking challenges present valuable opportunities for personal and professional development and self-exploration. Embrace your genuine identity and leverage psychological techniques to enhance your self-assurance and effectively impact others. Learn to overcome imposter syndrome and cultivate confidence in your abilities. It is important to remember that networking involves establishing sincere connections and maintaining authenticity are crucial for developing enduring relationships. Leverage psychological techniques to your benefit and adopt a proactive and self-assured attitude when engaging in networking activities.

9.2 Dealing with Rejection and Overcoming Fear

This section will discuss the art of gracefully handling rejection, cultivating self-acceptance, and boosting confidence to emanate charisma and charm in your networking efforts. Rejection is an opportunity for growth and resiliency, not a reflection of your worth. Let's examine methods for overcoming rejection, building self-assurance, and exuding magnetic charisma in your interactions.

Embracing Self-Acceptance: Self-acceptance is the key to overcoming rejection. Adopt the following behaviors to cultivate a positive self-image:

Replace Self Doubt with Self-assurance: Monitor your inner dialogue and replace self-doubting thoughts with self-affirming ones. Remind yourself of your accomplishments and strengths.

Learn from Rejection: Rather than ruminating on rejection, use it as an opportunity to learn and grow. Seek feedback and identify areas for improvement without self-criticism.

Surround Yourself with Supportive Individuals: Develop relationships with those who uplift and value you. During difficult circumstances, a solid social network can boost one's self-esteem.

Constructing Unshakeable Confidence:

- Confidence is magnetic and draws others to you. Here's how to develop unshakeable self-assurance:
- Imagine yourself confidently navigating networking events and establishing solid connections. Visualization can manifest self-assurance in the actual world.
- Define Attainable Networking Objectives and Commemorate Milestones. Recognize your development and proficiency.
- Concentrate on Your Strengths Recognize your skills and distinctive qualities. Capitalize on your unique qualities.
- Accept the adage, "You are what you think of yourself." Develop a positive self-image that is resistant to being undermined by negative comments.

Persuasion and Charisma Development

Charisma is the ability to captivate and persuade others. Enhance your appeal with the following techniques:

- Active Listening: Engage in active listening to demonstrate genuine concern for others. People gravitate toward those who make them feel valued and heard.
- A well-placed and tasteful sense of humor can lighten the mood and endear you to others.
- Exhibit Kindness and Empathy: Address conversations with warmth and sensitivity. Facilitate the exchange of thoughts and experiences by others.
- Be Present and Engaging: During conversations, focus on the present moment, sustain eye contact, and avoid distractions. Engage wholeheartedly with those with whom you interact.

Continuous Improvement Practice:

Like any other skill, networking improves with practice. Here is how to continually improve your networking skills:

- Participate in Diverse Events: Attend a variety of networking events and conferences. Each experience affords you the chance to hone your networking skills.
- Request Feedback: Request feedback on your networking style from trusted peers or mentors. Sincere feedback can illuminate development opportunities.
- Engage in Role Play: Rehearse networking scenarios with peers or coworkers to improve social and communication skills.

Rejection is an opportunity to embrace self-acceptance and develop unshakeable confidence. Remember that your value is not contingent upon external validation. Develop a self-image that negative comments cannot diminish. To become more charming and charismatic, engaging in active listening is essential, demonstrating sincerity and empathy, and using humor with discretion is important. Always look for opportunities to improve your networking abilities, and be receptive to learning from every interaction. With self-assurance and magnetic charisma, you'll easily navigate networking events, forming genuine connections that advance your personal and professional goals. Embrace the journey of continuous development and observe as your charismatic authenticity attracts others, fostering long-lasting and significant relationships.

9.3 Networking in a Virtual Environment

Accepting the Virtual Networking Experience Virtual networking is a crucial aspect of the contemporary professional world. Embrace its potential and implement the following strategies to maximize your success with virtual networking:

- Optimize Your Virtual Space: Ensure that your background is clean and professional. Position your camera at eye level during video calls to sustain eye contact.

- Familiarize yourself with online meeting platforms, messaging functions, and breakout rooms. Being technologically savvy will make you feel more comfortable at networking events.

- Even though you may be in the convenience of your own home, you should dress professionally to maintain a sense of professionalism and self-assurance.

- Create a Networking Schedule: Regularly plan and schedule opportunities for virtual networking. Consistency will assist you in gaining momentum and expanding your network.

The Importance of Personal Branding Online:

Virtual networking relies heavily on your online presence. Create a compelling online personal brand using the following strategies:

Ensure your LinkedIn profile is comprehensive and highlights your skills, experiences, and accomplishments. Utilize content pertinent to your industry to improve your visibility.

Curate Your Digital Footprint: Regularly audits your online presence and eliminates any content that could harm your professional reputation.

Thought leadership: Disseminate valuable insights and knowledge via blog posts, articles, and social media platforms. Position yourself as an industry thought leader.

Participate in virtual networking events hosted by professional associations, industry organizations, or online communities.

Engaging Authentically in Virtual Networking Creating meaningful connections through virtual networking requires authentic engagement. Employ these techniques for authentic engagement:

Active Listening: During virtual conversations, practice active listening. Display genuine curiosity in the viewpoints and experiences of others.

Customization: Tailor your approach to every virtual interaction. Refer to shared experiences or interests to establish rapport.

Emails vs. Video Calls: When practicable, choose video calls over emails to establish a more personal connection. In-person interactions foster trust and rapport.

Focus on fostering mutually beneficial relationships rather than pursuing immediate gains. Networking involves constructing a solid support system.

Transforming virtual relationships into actual ones:

With the proper care, virtual connections can blossom into real-world relationships. How to strengthen virtual ties:

After virtual networking events, promptly follow up with personalized messages. Refer to specific details of the conversation to demonstrate your interest.

Schedule Virtual Coffee Meetings: Transform virtual connections into deeper relationships by scheduling virtual coffee meetings individually.

Seek out opportunities for virtual collaborations and joint initiatives. The partnership strengthens bonds and promotes shared success.

Networking in a virtual setting requires adaptability, technological savvy, and genuine engagement. Embrace virtual networking opportunities and optimize your online personal brand to make an impression that lasts. Engage in virtual conversations with sincerity, concentrating on active listening and customization. Consolidate virtual relationships through prompt follow-up and virtual coffee meetings. Virtual networking has the potential to unite you with professionals from all over the world, transcending geographical boundaries. By mastering the art of connection in the digital sphere, you will expand your network, cultivate meaningful relationships, and gain access to exciting opportunities within your industry. Adopt virtual networking as a valuable component of your networking arsenal, and observe as your network flourishes in the digital age.

Key Takeaways from Chapter 9: Overcoming Challenges in Networking

Introversion and Making Friends:

- Accept that you are shy and use that as a skill.
- Focus on having deep talks with smaller groups. How to Handle Rejection:

- Always keep in mind that rejection is a normal part of networking.
- Use it as a way to learn and improve how you do things.

Creating connections in a virtual world:

- Be there and pay attention to master virtual networking.
- Use video calls to make real bonds with other people.

Acceptance of oneself and confidence:

- Accept yourself and have faith in your skills.
- If you know yourself, people will likely trust and connect with you.

How Mind Tricks Work:

- Use upbeat self-talk to help you feel better about networking.
- Imagine successful encounters to get in the right frame of mind.

Be Charming and charismatic:

- Be interested in other people to become more charming.
- Show warmth, understanding, and a good attitude when you talk to people.

How to Build Good Relationships:

- Focus on building trust and a good relationship with the people you know.
- Give help and support to create ties that will last.

Practice will make you better:

- Regularly practicing networking will help you get better at it.
- Start with more minor challenges and work up to bigger ones.

Accept Chances for Growth:

- Take on problems as a chance to learn and grow.
- Get out of your comfort zone and take advantage of opportunities to network.

Face problems with a smile and the desire to learn. Accept what makes you different and use that to build relationships. Don't forget that networking is a trip, and each new experience is a step toward your success!

Multiple Choice Questions

1. How can individuals overcome networking challenges related to introversion?

a) Avoid attending networking events to minimize social interactions.

b) Embrace their authentic selves and showcase genuine personality.

c) Pretend to be someone they are not to fit in with others.

d) Refrain from engaging in personal conversations during networking.

2. What is one psychological strategy to enhance self-assurance in networking scenarios?

a) Adopting power poses to feel disempowered and insecure.

b) Visualizing fruitful networking interactions and positive outcomes.

c) Avoiding setting attainable networking objectives to reduce pressure.

d) Focusing solely on the achievements and milestones of others.

3. How can networking challenges related to imposter syndrome be addressed effectively?

a) Acknowledging accomplishments and seeking supportive feedback.

b) Suppressing self-doubt and dismissing one's achievements.

c) Concentrating solely on showcasing abilities and accomplishments.

d) Refusing to participate in networking events due to lack of confidence.

4. What is one technique to positively influence others during networking interactions?

a) Avoiding mirroring techniques to establish a sense of familiarity.

b) Demonstrating active listening and asking open-ended questions.

c) Withholding genuine compliments and validation to maintain distance.

d) Neglecting to engage in meaningful conversations with others.

5. How can individuals handle rejection gracefully in networking?

a) Ruminating on rejection and engaging in self-criticism.

b) Avoiding seeking feedback and learning from rejection experiences.

c) Embracing self-acceptance and using rejection as a growth opportunity.

d) Surrounding themselves with individuals who criticize their skills.

6. What is one strategy for constructing unshakeable confidence during networking?

a) Imagining oneself as a disheartened and unaccomplished networker.

b) Focusing solely on weaknesses and disregarding strengths.

c) Setting unattainable networking objectives to reduce confidence.

d) Concentrating on personal strengths and accomplishments.

7. How can individuals foster authentic engagement in virtual networking?

a) Avoiding customization and generic interactions in virtual conversations.

b) Neglecting to employ active listening during virtual interactions.

c) Focusing solely on email communications instead of video calls.

d) Demonstrating sincere curiosity and engagement in viewpoints of others.

8. Why is personal branding significant in the context of virtual networking?

a) To maintain a negative online presence that showcases authenticity.

b) To neglect curating one's digital footprint and personal image.

c) To ensure one's LinkedIn profile lacks relevant skills and accomplishments.

d) To create a compelling online personal brand that enhances visibility.

9. How can individuals transform virtual connections into real-world relationships?

a) Delaying follow-up messages after virtual networking events.

b) Ignoring opportunities for virtual collaborations and joint initiatives.

c) Promptly following up with personalized messages and scheduling virtual coffee meetings.

d) Exclusively engaging in virtual interactions without pursuing in-person meetings.

10. Why is continuous improvement practice essential in networking?

a) To limit networking opportunities to a specific event or conference.

b) To avoid seeking feedback from peers and mentors.

c) To solely rely on in-person networking without virtual engagement.

d) To develop networking skills through diverse events and role-playing.

Answers

1. b

2. b

3. a

4. b

5. c

6. d

7. d

8. d

9. c

10. d

Chapter 10: Networking for Career Advancement

In the ever-evolving and cutthroat advertising, media, and entertainment industries, cementing one's position as a frontrunner in the field is crucial. Strategic and authentic networking can be a game-changer for accomplishing these goals. This chapter examines how networking may boost your professional profile, increase your demand, and establish credibility.

"The richest people in the world look for and build networks, everyone else looks for work." - Robert Kiyosaki

10.1 Leveraging Networking for Professional Development

Recognizability and prominence in the dynamic and cutthroat media, entertainment, and advertising sectors can lead to remarkable opportunities and career advancement. You may accomplish these objectives and raise your profile in the media and industry by engaging in productive networking. In this chapter, we will go deep into networking and how it can help you become well-known in your profession, gain the trust of your peers and clients, and broaden your circle of influential contacts.

Creating a Personal Brand for Yourself: To succeed in a competitive field, you need a solid personal brand as the cornerstone of your professional identity. You may mold and expand your brand with the help of networking.

Consistency Is Crucial: Maintain uniformity in your brand's messaging across all mediums, from social media to in-person events.

Showing off Knowledge: Join discussions about your field, offer helpful advice, and post insightful articles to build your reputation as an expert.

To become a thought leader in your field, you need to cultivate an original outlook on your area's issues and participate in discussions about those issues.

A solid online presence can help you get noticed and boost the demand for your services or products.

The best **LinkedIn strategies** involve highlighting your most impressive professional qualities. Join industry-specific communities and network with other professionals.

Get involved in social media by posting your ideas, updates in your field, and peeks of your work in progress on sites like Twitter, Instagram, and YouTube.

Making Useful Content: Content is a great way to show off your knowledge and attract new followers.

Start a blog where you can discuss your area of expertise, share your experiences, and offer advice to others. You can consider launching a YouTube channel or making industry-specific films to reach a larger audience. Increasing your visibility and demand in your field through public speaking engagements and thought leadership. Conferences, seminars, and workshops are all great places to meet others in your area and share what you've learned.

Showcase your knowledge and make connections with a broader audience by hosting webinars or appearing as a guest on relevant podcasts.

Building Trust and Lasting Partnerships Networking is about making real, lasting connections.

Establishing rapport requires genuine curiosity in others, listening attentively, and looking for areas of shared interest outside of work. Don't expect anything in return if you offer help, resources, or introductions. You can raise your profile considerably by participating in trade shows, conferences, and other events. Join professional organizations in your field and become involved with the activities they host. Attend and participate in industry conferences to network with thought leaders and colleagues. Although networking is not exclusive to the media sector, developing relationships with journalists can increase your profile. To network with reporters, producers, and opinion leaders, participate in media-centric gatherings, including conferences, workshops, and celebrations.

Collaborative efforts: team up with influential people in the media to multiply your reach and effect.

Making new connections, expanding your professional reach, and gaining the respect of your fellows and clients are all possible thanks to networking. You can become a recognized authority in your profession if you invest time and effort into developing a solid personal brand, taking advantage of opportunities to gain exposure online, and publishing high-quality material. You can increase your visibility in your field and broaden your reach by giving talks, cultivating genuine relationships, and attending conferences and other events.

Consistency, sincerity, and passion for your sector will be the cornerstone of your success as you establish your reputation and influence through networking. Your personal brand will thrive, and your impact will expand in the media, entertainment, and advertising industries if you put time and effort into cultivating genuine relationships and providing value to people. Networking is a robust tool that may help you advance in your career, gain exposure, and establish yourself as a thought leader if you commit to using it. Achieving prominence as a market leader requires making just one connection. Best of luck in your networking endeavors!

10.2 Exploring New Opportunities and Job Searching

There's more o networking than just collecting business cards at events; it's about building meaningful connections that might lead to breakthroughs in your professional life. In this chapter, learn how to use networking to your advantage as you seek new chances and navigate the competitive job market in the media, entertainment, and advertising sectors.

Connecting with People in Your Niche:

In addition to attending big conventions, you should also look for more intimate, niche gatherings to network at. Participate in media, entertainment, and advertising-related online forums, discussion groups, and social media communities. When you interact with others who share your interests and expertise, you increase your chances of making valuable connections, gaining new perspectives, and discovering exciting new opportunities for collaboration.

How to Get the Most Out of Your Informational Interviews

Informational interviews are a priceless resource for those seeking employment and those with experience in the field. Get in touch with people in your area who you look up to or would like to emulate. Consider the interviews a chance to research the sector, ask questions, and learn more about potential job openings. You might not only learn something useful but also develop some connections with influential people.

The Value of Opposite Mentoring for Personal Growth

Mentoring typically entails an established expert guiding an up-and-coming one. You might reverse the script and choose a mentor among the younger IT experts familiar with all the newest gadgets and software. This method of learning from those more experienced in your field will help you adapt to the ever-changing business landscape.

Group Work as an Opportunity to Display Your Talents

In today's competitive employment market, group projects can be an excellent method to demonstrate your skills to potential employers. Create short films, podcasts, or advertising campaigns with other artists and professionals in your field. These group projects are great opportunities to showcase your skills and build a portfolio that impresses future employers.

Making an Impression That Lasts Begins with Personalized Follow-Ups

Following up with the people you meet at networking events is essential. Make your follow-up messages more personable by referring to particular points from your interaction. This considerate method can make a great first impression and show your interest in the person.

Participate in Online Communities for Expanded Opportunities

Numerous online possibilities are made possible by modern networking technologies. Expand your professional sphere outside your immediate area by participating in webinars, online conferences, and other similar online events. Accept the benefits of online networking to maintain and expand your professional network.

Be interested and curious; keep learning.

Building professional and personal relationships through networking is more than meeting new people. Don't lose your sense of wonder about shifting norms, cutting-edge tools, and promising methods. Continuing your education will not only make you more useful in your field, but it will also give you material for conversation at professional events.

Connect with people from different backgrounds and experiences.

Possibilities and viewpoints can be expanded by connecting with people from different backgrounds. Make an effort to meet and network with people from various occupations, cultures, and backgrounds. Industries constantly change, so you must surround yourself with people who can help you keep up.

Coaching and Giving Back: Pass It On

Giving back to the next generation of professionals is essential as you climb the corporate ladder. Mentoring is a win-win situation since you help someone else develop while strengthening your knowledge and leadership abilities in your field. Volunteering as a mentor is a great way to give back to the community and create generational relationships in the workplace.

Let's discuss how networking can help your job hunt and boost your industry and media visibility.

- Use the Hidden Job Market: Professional networks share many job openings. Networking opens the secret job market, where referrals and word-of-mouth recommendations can lead to exclusive chances.

- Use networking to boost your internet profile. Your LinkedIn profile should reflect your career goals. Join industry-related social media debates to establish yourself as a thought leader and attract possible employers.

- Referrals are strong. Establishing genuine relationships increases your chances of being referred to employment openings or introduced to hiring managers.

- Informative Interviews for Career Insights: When networking, seek informational interviews with people in jobs or organizations you want to join. These chats can help you connect with industry decision-makers and gain professional insights.

- Industry Networking Recruiters: Attend industry-specific networking events. These events allow you to impress and possibly land interviews or jobs.

- Showcase Your Value: Networking lets you demonstrate your skills in a more casual situation. To impress potential employers, talk about your achievements and selling qualities.

- Job searchers can benefit from joining alum networks and industry-related professional groups. These networks offer job boards, career resources, and industry-specific events.

- Networking improves soft skills like communication, active listening, and relationship-building, which employers value. These abilities improve networking and professional marketability.

- Strategic Follow-Ups: Thank people after networking events or interviews. Thank them for connecting and restate your interest in job openings. Follow-ups show excitement and professionalism.

- Networking While Volunteering: Your industry might help you network while supporting a cause. Volunteering lets you meet industry peers and demonstrate your commitment.

- Networking Within Media Circles: The media industry lives on connections, and networking within media circles is highly beneficial. Attend media events, join online media networks, and seek mentorship from media experts.

- Attend industry conferences, workshops, and seminars. Panel discussions, presentations, hackathons, and creative competitions are great ways to be noticed.

Networking is an ongoing process with long-term benefits. Be genuine and persistent. Your network may help you discover jobs, shape your professional identity, boost skill demand, and establish you as an industry and media influencer—a network to achieve your job goals.

10.3 Sustaining Long-Term Relationships

Congratulations! You have arrived at this point in your journey because you have successfully learned to traverse the world of networking. The genuine value of networking comes from building and maintaining meaningful connections over time. This chapter explores the science and art of forming lasting bonds and the human factors contributing to healthy partnerships.

Authenticity is the bedrock of any long-lasting relationship, so be sure you're cultivating it. Follow your path and let your unique character emerge. Sincerity and openness attract others; they are more willing to interact with and support someone they perceive to be genuine.

Reciprocity is a powerful notion that influences how people connect. People are more likely to help and support you in return when you help and keep them. Relationships develop when you help one another out, pool resources, and rejoice in one another's achievements.

From a psychological standpoint, **Trust** is the bedrock of any lasting relationship. It takes effort and a long time to build trust. Be dependable, maintain your word, and always act honestly and honestly. Connections built on trust and honesty will likely last, and your peers will probably promote you.

Engage in careful listening; it's an art form that may strengthen your relationships. Active listening entails paying attention while the other person is talking and showing that you care about what they say. Having conversations that matter can help people feel closer and increase their respect for one another.

Try to agree on something: Find common ground in areas that aren't work-related, such as hobbies, sports, or causes. Personal interactions are the foundation of great relationships and lifelong friendships.

Be a giver and a taker in relationships; don't enter them thinking only of what you can get out of them. Instead, be willing to help others, share what you know, and lend a hand, even if you don't get anything in return. In the long run, those who are generous are rewarded for their efforts.

Networking and Emotional Intelligence: EI is the capacity to identify and effectively handle one's own and other people's emotional states. Developing your EI can help you cope with stress, resolve disagreements, and engage with others with optimism and compassion, even in adversity.

Maintaining connections requires **regular contact and a commitment** to being consistent. Keep in touch with your network consistently through email updates, in-person get-togethers, or online discussions. Maintaining a steady stream of contact demonstrates that you care about keeping the relationship strong.

Acknowledge and celebrate the accomplishments and landmarks reached by your network. Please send your best wishes on their recent promotions, job anniversaries, or other achievements. Your friendship and sense of camaraderie will both benefit from celebrating together.

Serve as a bridge between those in your network. Partnerships and chances for collaboration can be fostered by introducing the right people to each other. You can increase your worth and gain a reputation as a peacemaker simply by being a connector.

Respect the boundaries of your relationships by keeping your distance when necessary. Not everyone may enjoy constant interaction or divulging private information. Always respect the personal space of others and pay attention to signs that someone needs space.

Professional relationships that provide emotional support are rare in today's fast-paced business world. However, showing compassion and offering help in times of need can strengthen bonds and foster a feeling of community in your network.

Long-term friendships result from hard work, compassion, and genuine interest in the other person. The more you put in the effort to build these relationships, the more helpful they will become to you professionally and in your pursuit of happiness. So, go out there and cultivate your connections; they can help you in ways you can't even imagine, personally and professionally.

Multiple Choice Questions

1. How can individuals raise their professional profile in the media and entertainment industries through networking?

a) By avoiding social media and in-person events to maintain privacy.

b) Creating a solid personal brand and showcasing expertise through content.

c) Disregarding the importance of online presence and thought leadership.

d) Limiting interactions to large conventions and avoiding niche gatherings.

2. What is a valuable strategy to gain exposure online and attract potential employers?

a) Staying anonymous and avoiding participation in social media debates.

b) Sharing work in progress on personal social media accounts.

c) Neglecting to post insightful articles and industry-specific content.

d) Joining industry-related communities and showcasing knowledge.

3. What can individuals do to explore new opportunities and navigate the competitive job market effectively?

a) Attend only large industry conferences and overlook niche gatherings.

b) Disregard informational interviews as they offer little value.

c) Engage in opposite mentoring to improve soft skills.

d) Participate in group projects to demonstrate their skills and build a portfolio.

4. Why are personalized follow-ups essential after networking events or interviews?

a) To show disinterest in building lasting connections.

b) To make a lasting impression and demonstrate genuine interest.

c) To avoid appearing too eager or enthusiastic about potential opportunities.

d) To assert superiority over others and maintain a sense of authority.

5. How can individuals expand their professional reach beyond their immediate area?

a) By limiting networking to in-person events and avoiding online opportunities.

b) Engaging in online communities, webinars, and virtual conferences.

c) Restricting connections to individuals from the same background and experiences.

d) Focusing solely on building relationships within their own industry.

6. Which of the following is a crucial factor contributing to healthy and long-lasting partnerships in networking?

a) Deceptiveness and projecting a false persona.

b) Consistency in networking efforts and follow-ups.

c) Avoiding reciprocity to avoid feeling obligated.

d) Disregarding emotional intelligence in networking interactions.

7. What is one way to foster trust in networking relationships?

a) By being inconsistent and unreliable in interactions.

b) Maintaining honesty and acting with integrity.

c) Avoiding personal interactions and engagement.

d) Demonstrating indifference to others' achievements and milestones.

8. How can individuals demonstrate active listening during networking interactions?

a) By interrupting and dominating the conversation.

b) Showing curiosity and care while others are speaking.

c) Ignoring others' viewpoints and experiences.

d) Avoiding discussions outside of work-related topics.

9. Why is reciprocity an important concept in networking relationships?

a) It creates an obligation to give without expecting anything in return.

b) It fosters a competitive atmosphere and undermines trust.

c) It leads to a one-sided relationship where only one party benefits.

d) It encourages individuals to prioritize their own needs above others'.

10. What is the value of participating in group projects in the competitive job market?

a) Group projects are time-consuming and have little impact on employers.

b) They demonstrate collaborative skills and build an impressive portfolio.

c) Group projects are insignificant in comparison to individual achievements.

d) Employers are not interested in candidates with a diverse skill set.

Answers

1. b

2. d

3. d

4. b

5. b

6. b

7. b

8. b

9. d

10. b

Conclusion:

Congratulations! You've taken the first step on a life-changing adventure via "Network Like a Pro." At this point in the guide, I would like to thank you very much for following along with me. I have dedicated my life to writing this book so that others may benefit from the knowledge and wisdom I have earned from years of working in media, entertainment, and advertising.

We have spent this entire book debunking fallacies about networking and examining its potential benefits. By thinking carefully about where you want to go, who you want to connect with, and what you want to say to them, we've laid solid groundwork for your future success.

You now know how to do your homework before a networking event, where to find relevant information, and how to give a compelling elevator speech. Effective networking techniques have been discussed, focusing on active listening, making an impact, and maintaining genuine connections.

Online networking platforms like LinkedIn are increasingly crucial in today's digital world, and we've discussed how to make the most of them to boost your career profile. You now have the knowledge and experience to participate confidently and benefit from online networking opportunities.

The potential for cross-departmental collaboration and establishing ties with leaders and mentors has been revealed, revealing the power of internal networking within your firm. We have broadened our horizons by engaging in activities outside your organization, such as joining a trade group, attending a conference, or volunteering.

You can now conquer these obstacles and achieve your networking goals, whether it's shyness, rejection, or the unfamiliarity of online social circles. You've perfected the art of small conversation and learned how to transform superficial interactions with strangers into genuine bonds.

And as you move forward in your networking adventure, remember that genuineness, reciprocity, and emotional intelligence are the keys to building and maintaining meaningful connections that last. Honor the achievements of your contacts, stand by them in times of difficulty, and keep being the bridge that connects people.

As we part ways, I hope you remember that genuine connection between people is at the core of effective networking. It's not about using one another to get what you want. You've gained the self-assurance and communication skills necessary to initiate a conversation with anyone, regardless of rank, and pique their attention enough to warrant further contact.

Keep in mind that you are the one responsible for your achievements. Your network is your most valuable resource, and the connections you make along the road will affect your trip in ways you can't even begin to fathom right now. Never pass on a chance conversation that might lead to a great collaboration or even a lasting friendship; it could change the course of your life.

I appreciate you being a part of something so life-altering. I hope you succeed in all you do and make many beautiful relationships along the way. I hope the relationships you build are the bedrock upon which you build your career and realize your goals.

You are destined for greatness, so go out there and network like a pro.

Useful References:

Chapter 1

1. Dunbar, R. I. M. (1993). "Co-evolution of neocortex size, group size and language in humans." Behavioral and Brain Sciences, 16(4), 681-735

2. Cialdini, R. B. (2001). "Influence: Science and Practice." Allyn & Bacon.

3. Goleman, D. (1995). "Emotional Intelligence: Why It Can Matter More Than IQ." Bantam Books.

Chapter 2

1. Myers, D. G., & Diener, E. (1996). "The Pursuit of Happiness." Scientific American, 274(5), 54-58.

2. Bargh, J. A., & McKenna, K. Y. A. (2004). "The Internet and Social Life." Annual Review of Psychology, 55, 573-590.

3. Caprariello, P. A., & Reis, H. T. (2013). "To do, to have, or to share? Valuing experiences over material possessions depends on the involvement of others." Journal of Personality and Social Psychology, 104(2), 199-215.

Chapter 3

1. Duckworth, A. L., Peterson, C., Matthews, M. D., & Kelly, D. R. (2007). "Grit: Perseverance and passion for long-term goals." Journal of Personality and Social Psychology, 92(6), 1087-1101.

2. Cacioppo, J. T., & Patrick, W. (2008). "Loneliness: Human nature and the need for social connection." W. W. Norton & Company.

3. Baumeister, R. F., & Leary, M. R. (1995). "The need to belong: Desire for interpersonal attachments as a fundamental human motivation." Psychological Bulletin, 117(3), 497-529.

Chapter 4

1. Reis, H. T., & Shaver, P. (1988). "Intimacy as an interpersonal process." Handbook of personal relationships, 367-389.

2. Baumeister, R. F., Vohs, K. D., & Funder, D. C. (2007). "Psychology as the science of self-reports and finger movements: Whatever happened to actual behavior?" Perspectives on Psychological Science, 2(4), 396-403.

3. Berscheid, E., & Reis, H. T. (1998). "Attraction and close relationships." The handbook of social psychology, 2, 193-281.

Chapter 5

1. Bavelas, J. B., Black, A., Lemery, C. R., & Mullett, J. (1986). "I show how you feel: Motor mimicry as a communicative act." Journal of personality and social psychology, 50(2), 322.

2. Burgoon, J. K., & Le Poire, B. A. (1999). "Nonverbal cues and interpersonal judgments: Participant and observer perceptions of intimacy, dominance, composure, and formality." Communication Monographs, 66(2), 105-124.

3. Gottman, J. M. (1994). "What predicts divorce? The relationship between marital processes and marital outcomes." Hillsdale, NJ: Lawrence Erlbaum Associates.

Chapter 6

1. Bandura, A. (1977). "Self-efficacy: Toward a unifying theory of behavioral change." Psychological Review, 84(2), 191-215.

2. Dweck, C. S. (2006). "Mindset: The New Psychology of Success." New York: Random House.

3. Lazarus, R. S., & Folkman, S. (1984). "Stress, appraisal, and coping." New York: Springer.

Chapter 7

1. Cialdini, R. B. (2009). "Influence: Science and Practice." Boston: Pearson Education.

2. Deci, E. L., & Ryan, R. M. (2000). "The 'what' and 'why' of goal pursuits: Human needs and the self-determination of behavior." Psychological Inquiry, 11(4), 227-268.

3. Goleman, D. (1995). "Emotional Intelligence: Why It Can Matter More Than IQ." New York: Bantam Books.

Chapter 8

1. Bandura, A. (1977). "Self-efficacy: Toward a unifying theory of behavioral change." Psychological Review, 84(2), 191-215.

2. Dweck, C. S. (2006). "Mindset: The New Psychology of Success." New York: Random House.

3. Kahneman, D. (2011). "Thinking, Fast and Slow." New York: Farrar, Straus, and Giroux.

Chapter 9

1. Reis, H. T., & Gable, S. L. (2000). "Toward a Positive Psychology of Relationships." In C. R. Snyder & S. J. Lopez (Eds.), "Handbook of Positive Psychology" (pp. 129-143). New York: Oxford University Press.

2. Baumeister, R. F., & Leary, M. R. (1995). "The Need to Belong: Desire for Interpersonal Attachments as a Fundamental Human Motivation." Psychological Bulletin, 117(3), 497-529.

3. Gottman, J. M. (1994). "What Predicts Divorce? The Measures." Hillsdale, NJ: Lawrence Erlbaum Associates.

Chapter 10

1. Baumeister, R. F., & Leary, M. R. (1995). "The Need to Belong: Desire for Interpersonal Attachments as a Fundamental Human Motivation." Psychological Bulletin, 117(3), 497-529.

2. Cacioppo, J. T., & Patrick, W. (2008). "Loneliness: Human Nature and the Need for Social Connection." New York: W. W. Norton & Company.

3. Cialdini, R. B. (2001). "Influence: Science and Practice." New York: Pearson.

4. Gladwell, M. (2000). "The Tipping Point: How Little Things Can Make a Big Difference." New York: Little, Brown, and Company.